Karma Rules

By

Arthur Ball

www.karmarules.com

Printed in the United States of America

Contents

Karma Rules

Introduction

This book was written to share with you the things I have learned from over twenty-five years of study and introspective thought. The universe provides the questions and the answers. All we need do is ask.

My spiritual journey started as a result of a dream I had. I was agonizing about a stock I owned. I bought it at a higher price than it was currently trading for and was trying to decide whether to sell it or keep it. My thinking was, "If I keep it, it could go back up and I'd be financially redeemed." But on the other hand, if it went down in price, it would be worth even less. So the dilemma of what to do was causing me a great deal on anxiety.

One night I had a dream about the stock. It was like seeing a slide show. This picture formed and I saw the stock prices as they would appear in the newspaper. The information was displayed before me with an isolation or focus on this one issue like it appeared in the newspaper. The information that was displayed showed vital details, like what price the stock closed at the day before, what price it opened at for the new day, how many total shares traded for the day, etc.

But the key number was the last bit of information. It was what the stock price had closed at for that day. The closing price was displayed with a "U" next to the amount indicating a new 52-week high had been achieved. The price shown was above the current price the stock was trading at by a fair amount.

The dream was so profound for me that as soon as I awoke that morning, I told my wife about it. I told her I was not going to sell the stock, as it would be going back up.

Within 90-days the dream came true. The stock performed exactly as I saw it in the dream. I was *so* amazed. How could a person see a future event? How could this happen? How could this be controlled? I went to the bookstore to see what books I could find on physic powers and how to gain control over them. I thought this would be a powerful tool if you could have this experience anytime you wanted to. On command.

Seeing the future is no doubt a powerful ability, and I wanted to be able to do it at will. Up until this event/experience, I never had a physic experience like this or any other type.

So I started reading every book I could find that dealt with the subject of physic powers. I read a variety of books for about a year. Even after that short amount of time I discovered that the various authors were presenting a single idea. To accomplish what I wanted to do, I would have to be in the moment. I had to be aware of the moment, with my consciousness focused in the moment of *now*. I had to be able to control my mind.

My awareness needed to be developed to the point where I could walk into a room, survey the contents, leave the room and be able to tell you what objects filled the space of that room. The different exercises that were proposed in the books were all about developing stronger mental control over the mind and senses. The goal was to raise ones awareness by being completely in the moment, all of the time.

Most of the books I read were purchased from the bookstores that were close to where I lived. I also liked to go to our local swap meet to see what treasures I might find. It was on one of these visits that I found a new book. It appeared to be just another book like the other ones I had been reading. It was titled *Messages From Michael*. As it turned out, it was nothing like the other books I had been reading.

It was a book about a group of people that were communicating with a spiritual entity named Michael. They were channeling the answers to the questions they were asking about different spiritual issues. Michael was actually a group of spirits they had been able to contact through their Ouija board.

The questions they were asking were quite profound. They wanted answers to the age-old questions many human beings have been asking for thousands of years. Why are we here? What is the purpose of life? How does life work? What are the laws that govern this planet and the human experience?

This was some seriously heavy stuff. The main point l liked about this book was the author's repeated recommendation to not just accept this information as fact, but to do other reading and validate the ideas being presented.

I was about a fourth of the way through it when I found myself saying, "This is about god." At that time in my life I can tell you that I thought the whole idea of God was a bunch of crap. I could not imagine that the God being talked about in church would allow all of the horrible things to take place that are a part of daily life on earth.

Raised in the Catholic Church, I had attended some bible study and in my youth had completed my first Holy Communion. My mother provided only a limited amount of guidance in spiritual matters.

My father divorced my mother when I was around three years old. My mother was both the father and the mother figure; she took up the roll of breadwinner. My mother did not have

8

much time for traditional parenting as she was working from ten to twelve hours per day, six days a week.

I formed my ideas about God as so many people do. My idea came from the people around me who had an influence on my life and what I picked up from school, church, individuals, newspapers and television, etc. I believe the biggest influence on my idea of what God was or was not came from all of the things that make life, Life. For example, the violent acts that the media just loves to report, and the pain and suffering that is going on throughout the world.

I remember one of my mother's favorite things to tell us at the dinner table: "There are starving children in China and we should eat every bite of food that was on our plate, because we are so lucky to have the food." She was right, at that time there were people starving in China. I would ask, "How can God let this happen?"

The *Michael* book changed the direction of my reading from a pursuit of knowledge about physic powers to a pursuit of spiritual knowledge. I was so intrigued by what I read in the *Michael* book. It presented God and the idea of being a human in such a really different way. I was fascinated by the new ideas presented about what life was about and how it worked. I was amazed to learn there are laws that govern the entire universe and the human experience. That life is not a series of accidental possibilities, but a controlled evolving plan. That things are interrelated and there is peace harmony and love in the universe. Ideas of this type were not part of my world. This was new and exciting information.

I was fortunate to be making a good living at that time from the company I owned, so I was able to travel frequently and thus had a great deal of time to read. My wife and I went on a number of vacations to nice resorts and we would just hang out on the beach and read.

I also owned a boat that allowed me to go to Catalina Island, off the coast of Southern California, on a regular basis. We would moor the boat at a place called the Isthmus and just enjoy the serene surroundings. That gave me even more time to read, as all we did was relax. I would read between fifteen and twenty books a year. I was only reading books on the subject of Life.

My ideas started to change about God and what life really was and what it was not. I remember thinking that if I was going to learn, I would need to tell myself, "I now know nothing, I will accept everything I read without judgment, but will not make it a belief. I will make it an understanding, until some new information is presented that either makes more sense or is validated through repetition."

When one has beliefs, those beliefs can close the door on new information. We do not want to disturb the comfort that goes with our beliefs. Everything is very neat and tidy and we have a tendency to not want to disturb or change the ideas we are comfortable with.

I feel the truth of an idea comes when it is presented from various sources, repetitiously, over a span of time. All of those different, intelligent, great minds, over thousands of years, could not be wrong.

I would ask the universe for guidance to lead me to the books with the answers to the questions that kept building, to guide me in my pursuit of knowledge. I wanted answers to the age-old questions. What is the purpose of life? Why are we here? How does life work? What are the laws that govern us? One question would lead to another and then another.

It seemed the questions kept growing and greatly outnumbered the answers. It is so incredible how universal consciousness can be tapped. If you ask, you *will* receive. Information will just come to you; it is like a knowing. We really can talk to God. We are definitely connected.

We are a part of universal consciousness and thus can communicate with it. Much of what I have learned has come to me through this method. At one time it was called channeling. It is a psychic gift other members of my family have been given. My great grandmother was a medium.

I focused my reading on anything and everything that had to do with Life. Books on religion, science, philosophy, psychology and the new age spiritual ideas, that were not new at all. The reading took on a life of its own. One book would lead to another and then another. It was like I was being lead by someone or something down a path.

The book's teachings spanned a great deal of time. From what Buddha taught more than twenty-five hundred years ago, through hundreds of years of great people, up to the present day. Most of the great ideas of what life is, or is not; was presented by philosophers and scientists. I was reading what people like Jesus Christ, Buddha, Plato, Socrates, Bacon, Carl Jung and other great minds thought life was about over hundreds of years.

What intrigued me the most is the pattern of consistency in what many of these great minds had to say about what life is and how it works. They might say it a little differently, but they were describing life's experiences and what the laws were in a very similar manner. I was sure that the continuity of an idea being presented over thousands of years, by different people, must be a Truth. The key was to not get locked into an idea or to judge it, but just accept everything until proven to be incorrect or not quite in that shape. An idea of what life is can be looked at as having a shape, like a circle or a square. So as I read more about the different ideas the shape would change. New information or old information presented in a different way would then alter my understanding of a spiritual idea or concept.

Discussing these different ideas with other people proved to be a bit frustrating, as most of the people I met that were interested in talking about this subject had opinions that did not have a foundation from study. Most of them were interested, but not enough to do much reading. It was hard to find knowledgeable people who were actually studying the subject of human life and spirituality.

I really tried not to get one idea so set in my understanding that I would close out new ideas that were in contradiction with the earlier concepts. On a couple of occasions I did reject an idea that was new. I can remember thinking "this cannot be true." Yet in every case the new idea proved to be accurate. That showed me how dangerous blocking out new information would be just because it was new and I had never been exposed to it before.

If I wasn't careful I could possibly block out something that was important, so I needed to remain open to new information. My growth and pursuit of knowledge was going to be limited if I did not let a new idea have a chance. Being non-judgmental was the only way to grow. This is a real challenge for each of us.

I found the knowledge I was gaining was changing the way I understood the events of life. It changed the experience of these events and the way I lived my life. The new information was changing how I either responded or reacted to the events that were taking place daily. It was like the knowledge was a filter between the events of life and me, and the filter was my understanding of what life was or was not.

It was incredible how my ideas about life influenced how I lived my life and how I evaluated the experiences. It was like I saw what I looked for. It was a tremendous challenge to accept things as they were, not how I though they should be. My ideas of life were coloring my experiences of life.

One of the biggest influences on my thinking was an idea that was presented while I was reading about Buddhism. The term Karma kept coming up. As I learned about a new idea or concept, it seemed the universe would bring me a number of books about that subject. It was like some outside source was controlling my education.

So let's start with what is by far the biggest and most important idea that I have found that influences our human experience, Karma.

CHAPTER ONE:
KARMA

Karma is the universal law of cause and effect.

This law is the main force that governs and influences each and every one of our lives.

The purpose of this law, as it pertains to the human experience, is to teach us through direct experience and to help us grow consciously. It does this by showing us the opposite side of our acts/cause. When we do something/cause, that act creates an effect/event in our lives. The effect/event does not have to occur in the present/current lifetime.

Let's say you strike someone in the face. The karma of that act would be that you would then be struck in the face by someone. Not necessarily the person you struck. It would probably be by someone else at a different time, although it could be by the person you struck, right then.

Karma is absolute. It is not arbitrary. An effect cannot be changed, once a cause has been initiated. This is what makes it a universal law.

Universal laws provide the order the universe must have to exist. The laws do not change from one day to the next or from year to year. They function the same for all of time. That is what makes them a universal law.

This higher power (God/Universal Consciousness) does not micro-manage the universe. This incredible consciousness has set laws in place that keeps everything working within the plan and I believe there is a plan.

I have read and heard that some people think one's Karma can be changed. This is not true. If we could change the law then it would not be a universal law. A thought will not create karma. Karma can only come from one's actions. We must do something to create a cause, which will then create an effect.

Another universal law is gravity; you cannot change how this law works. The universal laws do not change because someone would like it to be different, or they are sorry for something they have done. Being sorry for an act we have committed is not going to eliminate or change the karma from the act. Praying for forgiveness is not going to change the karma of an act. Karma is not about retribution.

The universal laws are set in place to provide order to the flow of the universe. They do not change from day-to-day. The universal laws are what guide our solar system through the vastness of the universe. The laws keep our planet and the other planets in their orbits. The laws are in place to keep the order that is necessary to keep everything from crashing into each other. The laws work with the same consistency over billions of years. That is what makes them universal laws.

It is important that we really grasp this concept, we *cannot change* our karma once it has been set in place by a cause/act.

So how does this Law of Karma influence our lives?

It is everything! Nothing happens in our life that is *not* part of our karma. There are no accidents. Things do not just "happen." We do not have good luck or bad luck. Some people are not more fortunate than others.

We all bring our individual karma into this life from the many previous lives we have lived. We are building our future every day. What we do, or do not do, during the course of each day is building our future karma.

All of the current events of our lives are the result of past karma. Our individual karma is what brings our daily experiences to us. What we have done in past lives and what we do in this life brings about the future events that come to us as experiences. (We will talk about reincarnation in a later chapter.)

Karma has no teeth without reincarnation being a fact. Life is not a one-time experience. We have lived many lives. The fact that we have lived many lives is what truly makes each of us human beings different. It is the main thing that influences our experience of life. The number of lives we have lived is called our Soul Age.

KARMA IS NOT ABOUT RETRIBUTION!
KARMA IS NOT ABOUT RETRIBUTION!

I will keep saying this over and over again.

Karma is about experiencing the opposite side of an act/cause and our moral code being developed from that experience, plus, we grow consciously from each experience. If this law did not provide these experiences we would continue to make poor choices. Knowledge of how the law works should make us think before we act. The moral code we live our life by, has been developed from the lessons/teachings, from the karma we have experienced in our past lives. Our individual moral code is constantly growing and expanding.

The law of karma gives us the opportunity to find out how it feels to be slapped back when we have struck someone. Without karma we might not have this experience. By experiencing the opposite side of our own acts, we get the growth and expansion of our moral values that is necessary to evolve consciously and make better choices.

If you find yourself saying, " I would not act like that or I would not be like that" you have learned from a past act. Karma has worked it's magic. The law of karma is what assists us in expanding the moral values we need to co-exist with other humans in a civilized society. In my mind, it is the most perfect law anyone could devise.

What could be more perfect than to get back everything that each of us gives out? What universal law or laws could be devised that would be more perfect? I suggest none. This law works for every act, both positive and negative, that each of us commits.

Karma shows us the importance of controlling our actions. To control our actions, we must learn to control our minds. Our actions come from our thoughts and instincts. Learning to control this process is extremely important if we want to live lives filled with peace and harmony.

The universal consciousness that governs all that is, is so profound in its depth of thought and ability to perceive relationships that we humans can barely relate to it. This consciousness is called many things: God, Allah, Higher Power, Universal Mind, Universal Consciousness, etc.

This profound consciousness has thought of everything we need to have a wonderful life on this planet. It has set governing laws in place to guide us through the total human experience. All we have to do is learn what the laws are, understand how they work and how they influence our lives, and then use the knowledge. God does not micro-manage the universe or we humans that are a part of it.

We humans are learning more everyday about how life works and how things are interrelated and connected. This new awareness comes to us because our consciousness is expanding with each new generation. Consciousness is what evolves; all else is part of the illusion.

I do not have the slightest doubt that karma is the main law that governs us as human beings, living the human experience. If karma was not a law and a fact, then I could not have had the dream about the stock and seen a future event. If things/events were not predestined, the dream could not have occurred.

Since that first dream I have had many more and in every case they have come true. I can always tell when a dream is an important one because I am awakened at the end with a sudden jolt. I have struggled to understand a few, but once I did they always came true. They will sometimes come to me as a metaphor.

It is the knowledge and understanding of this extremely important law that will make the most important difference/change in how we experience life. All of a sudden, there are no victims. There are no accidents. There is no good luck or bad luck. It is all perfect just as things happen and as life is, at any given moment.

We just have to use the knowledge and understanding of this law to change the way we experience and understand the events of life. When we use the knowledge of karma, we can now *respond* to life, rather than react to life. This is a powerful change in our awareness.

This new way of thinking will take a great deal of mental discipline every day. We must learn to see life through our karmic lenses. Once our understanding of this law is complete; we will never be victims again. Understanding this law will assist us in letting go of the *poor me* mentality or the feeling that life is treating us unfairly, or is picking on us. We will understand that each event of our life is our karma in action.

Let me tell you about some of the events of my life and how this new knowledge and awareness changed the way I viewed them. I realized that my experiencing of the events was making me grow in understanding and in becoming a better person. My value system was changing. The way I treated others was changing.

I may not like some of the things that were happening to me, but at least I let go of the idea that I was some kind of victim or that life was picking on me for no reason. It reduced the amount of whining I did and eventually eliminated it. It helped me understand the things that were happening to the people I knew.

One of the early events in my life occurred when I was a teenager. I was in high school and dating a girl. We had intercourse when we were 16-years old. You know how it is when you're young. We are trying everything out and experimenting, as most teenagers do. She got pregnant. When she told me she was pregnant we were both going out with someone else.

So we got married, it seemed like the right thing to do. Her parents were not happy with either of us. Her father did not come to the wedding ceremony. My mother was not too thrilled either. This marriage did last seventeen years and bore three wonderful children.

I had no professional skills at age sixteen. The only job I could get was in construction. I was a laborer. It was very hard work. So I decided to join the Navy when I turned seventeen. After completing boot camp and Communications School, I was assigned to an aircraft carrier. We were always going out to sea.

I had not been on the ship very long when it was deployed on a six-month cruise to visit various Asian ports. While I was gone, my wife lived in a small apartment with our son. We wrote letters and talked about how much we missed each other and loved each other.

When I returned from the cruise we had intercourse without protection. She was in such a hurry, I later found out why. It was not long before she informed me that she was pregnant again. But she would not see a doctor during the entire time she was pregnant. No matter what I said, she would not go to the doctor. Even her mother could not get her to go.

Seven months later she is had a baby. When I got to the hospital, (I was on the ship) I asked where women that had premature births were kept. The nurse informed me that my wife was with the women who went full-term. I was an eighteen-year-old, this news did not sink in for a while. I kept thinking something was not right. Why would she be with the full term women?

When I got to her room I asked her why she was with the women that had full-term pregnancies, if she was just seven months into her term? She then broke down and told me that she had gotten pregnant while I was gone and that she had a normal nine-month pregnancy.

As you can imagine, I was devastated. Her family was great to me during this time. My wife and I separated for a while, but after a few months we got back together. She put the baby up for adoption, as I was not going to parent this child. It was just too big of a reminder of her infidelity.

So what does my karma have to do with this event? I would have to have been a party to this type of experience in another life. I would have been someone who cheated on a spouse and inflicted a great deal of pain on them. I was now on the opposite side of this type of experience and was now the one in pain. It was my turn to find out how it feels to be hurt/betrayed by a spouse.

Karma is not about retribution!

Karma shows us the opposite side of a cause/act. That is all. Karma shows us what it is like to be the receiver, on the other side of an act/cause.

There was a child's death recently in San Diego that was highly publicized. A seven-year-old little girl was kidnapped from her home at night while her family slept. She was taken by a man and later murdered.

No one is more vulnerable than a young child. They cannot defend themselves against a bigger, stronger person, especially a man. They are at the mercy of any more powerful individual.

So what would be the karma of an event like this? Something like this touches a number of people in many different ways. For the little girl it was that she was the perpetrator of this type of act in another life. She now has to have the experience from the opposite side. She is now on the receiving end of this type of experience.

She was not a victim. It was her karma to be on the other side of this type of experience. We cannot protect our children from their karma, no matter how much we would like to. In another one of her lives, she was probably a male and committed this type of act.

It is not always easy to figure out what the Cause of an Effect was. For the most part, trying to figure out what one may have done to bring an experience into one's life does not matter and it serves no real purpose.

Understanding that we did do something in the past to bring an event into our life is important. It is the only way for us to understand that we are not victims when something negative occurs in our life that we do not like. It is not as challenging for us when the experience is a positive one.

The parents of this little girl have karma that gets in the middle of this too. They are experiencing a great deal of pain over this event. So what could be their karma surrounding this type of experience?

It could be that in one of their past lives, they perpetrated this type of crime against another human and they have already experienced being the receiver.

To really bring the totality of the pain from this type of act home to their consciousness, they are now involved in this event, but as the parents. They are just a little removed, as they are not harmed physically but certainly mentally and emotionally.

Another karmic situation that has intrigued me for a long time is what appears to happen to Jewish people. Look at the horrors Jewish people were put through during the Second World War; millions of them were murdered by Hitler. Even today they are subjected to a constant state of attack in Israel.

Why has this been their individual and group karma? It is not because they are being persecuted, either as individuals or as a race or religious group. Their karma as individuals and as a group of people, from *past acts*, has brought these events into their lives.

In past lives, these individuals initiated these acts, probably as a group, and they are now having the experience of being the receiver of these types of acts as individuals and as a group.

That is how karma works and how it influences our future lives. Our karma follows us from life to life. Death does not eliminate the effect from the cause once it has been set in motion. It stays with each of us until we burn the karma by having the opposite side of the experience. The effect must be experienced once a cause has been set in motion.

Racial prejudice is another good example of how karma will make a change in an individual's understanding of life. Suppose in a life an individual hates black people so much they do things against them, but do not physically harm them. In a future life, they will be Black, so they can experience first-hand how it feels to be hated because of their skin color.

If you see an individual experiencing some sort of prejudice against them, chances are they did these types of things to someone, at some time, in one of their past lives. Now it is their turn to experience prejudice. That is how Karma works. Karma teaches us through direct experience.

Karma is not about retribution; it is about directly experiencing the other side of an act. If you meet someone who has a prejudice against another race of people, you can bet you are dealing with a *younger soul*. Prejudice of any type is ignorance in action.

The easiest way to relate to this new way of karma thinking is to realize that we are not the body – we are only *in* it. We will talk more about this subject later.

We are dual consciousness beings, with a lower and higher consciousness. We are spiritual-energy beings in a spiritual-energy world.

Life may seem to create winners and losers, but that is not the case. It is always one's karma that creates the illusion of being a winner or a loser. The good luck or bad luck that befalls each of us is the result of our individual past karma. We have done something in a life that was a Cause, which created an Effect. We must now have the experience of the other side of the act, we must experience the Effect. Fortunately, it works both for the good things we do and the not so good.

A good friend of mine has some really great karma that is unfolding. She is in her late fifties. She is a hard-working woman who has struggled for most of her life to learn and to attain financial independence. She has a learning disorder that slows her down and makes learning more of a challenge. She has to work much harder than most people to accomplish her goals. She is currently an acupuncturist and also does massage. She earns most of her money from massage.

Three or four years ago she read about an acupuncturist in Arkansas that had developed a new technique to repair degenerative eyes. She was determined to learn this new process from the man who developed it. So she started calling him to try to get him to teach her the process he had developed.

She called him religiously every six months to find out when he was going to teach her this new process. After about four years of her steady calling, he agreed to teach her and some others. They eventually became business partners. He has been instrumental in setting her up in business. He has provided equipment, a Web site and even a few customers. He taught her the process and did not charge her a penny to do so. Her business is steadily growing.

This man has changed her life from one of financial weakness to financial strength. She is in a transition from a position of want, to one of abundance. Her karma finally took a turn for the better. It is obviously time for her to have a new experience with a stronger more positive financial perspective. Will it be better? Time will tell.

It is amazing how one's karma can change so quickly. We have a tendency to go along from one day to the next without anything really changing and then all of a sudden, Wham! Something comes from out of nowhere to completely alter the course of our life and steer it down a different path. One little decision can make a huge change in the direction of our lives. It is all the result of our karma at work; our karma steers us through life to have the experiences we are here to have.

Our karma, and thus our lives, have a flow. Our karma is leading us from one experience to the next, through the events that occur. Try not to resist the flow, or the events. Try to understand that the events we are experiencing are happening so we can gain from them. Our moral value system will expand and we will grow consciously from each experience.

Getting back to my friend, the fact that this man agreed to teach her this new procedure is huge. That one decision on his part changed her life, perhaps for the remainder of her life. Having the patients to watch our karma unfold can be a real challenge. We are all very impatient to have the life we imagine should be ours, right now!

I have another friend, Wanda who is in her forties. She has a mother who is *very* controlling. The karma Wanda has set in place during a past life to learn and grow from is so amazing, her story goes something like this.

She was an only child and part of a pretty small family group. As a child her mother dictated every aspect of her life in great detail. Her mother is a person who sees things as either black or white. There is a proper way to do everything.

Wanda moved out of the house and went to college. She never returned to live with her parents as an adult. When Wanda was around thirty years old, her parents got divorced, so she now had two separate relationships with them. Not long after the divorce her father passed away, so it was now just Wanda and her mother. She was an only child.

Wanda's mother wants to control every aspect of her life. She criticizes the clothes she wears, how she takes care of her pet, how she combs her hair. Absolutely every facet of her life is up for scrutiny and criticism.

Wanda has put herself on the opposite side of a very controlling parent to experience how it feels to be controlled. In one of her previous lives she was the controlling parent. Now it is her turn to grow and learn from this experience. She will probably not be a controlling person again in her next life or any other life.

This type of reversing of roles is the way karma teaches us to be better humans. There is no better experience, than being on the opposite side of the acts we perpetuate, to give us a new perspective on what the best behavior is, as a human.

My 29-year old nephew is going out with a girl who is 24-years old. She is nice and is making him very happy. At age 22, within a two-week period she went blind in one eye. The doctors have not been able to figure out why. She also developed skin cancer on her back at about the same time.

So what was this karma all about? I am not absolutely sure, but you can bet it had something to do with her being responsible for someone losing his or her sight in a past life. That is how karma works. Karma helps us to understand those events in life for which we do not otherwise have answers.

It is not always easy to understand the cause of an experience, but understanding the cause is not important.

Knowing that you or someone else involved in an experience is not a victim, is the most important point. As it says in the Bible, "You will reap what you sow!"

Take some time to reflect on your own life. What has transpired so far? What types of events have happened and what type of situations have you been exposed to that you did not enjoy? Maybe there are only really good events up to this point in your life? All of our life's experiences are about our individual karma, which leads to the growth of our consciousness and the expansion of our individual moral codes (learning to be a better human being).

There are many ways our individual karma dictates the path of our lives. All of the marriages, divorces, our children, relationships with others, jobs, finances, etc., are about our karma. The entire path from birth to death is the result of our karma. All of the major events and all of the minor events in our lives are the result of our karma in action.

We write the script for a life before we get here on earth – this reality – to have the experiences that burn the karma we have built up in past lives. It will include both the good and the not so good that we need to experience. We choose the experiences (karma) for the current life we are living, that we want to be a part of this life, for our moral growth and conscious evolution. Our lives are not a series of random accidents and possibilities

We have made the choices to have the experiences that have occurred and will occur in this life. We decided, not someone else. This new understanding can make such a huge difference in how we think about what is currently happening in our lives and what has happened in our past.

Our lives are the result of the karma we bring with us from one life to the next. Our karma brings the experiences of our life to us. It is like our life is a plate; our karma puts the food/events we are here to eat/have on our plate. We choose what this life's experiences will be and all that we are here to learn. We are never victims.

If our lives are not what we want, we have no one to blame for the lives we are living but ourselves. We have created the circumstances through past acts that put us where we are today. Just examine how you live your life right now. Are you a model human being? Are you totally honest all of the time? Do you treat everyone with love and compassion? Do you live a life full of integrity? Do you respect your fellow human? How are you living this life?

REMEMBERING PAST LIVES

Why don't we remember past lives? In a sense we do. All of the past experiences from our other lives are the "common sense" we have. Two major examples include our value system that is in place that we use to make our choices every day, and the things we just seem to *know* about life.

The lack of prejudices in some people and not in others is a good example of this remembering. The more lives we live, the more we understand that we are all a part of the same family, no matter what our race, gender, sexual preference, country of origin or religion. Our individual soul age shows up in so many ways, in *who we are, how we think* and *how we treat other people.*

Remembering the details of our past lives is of no real value. It serves no real purpose. Karma takes care of teaching us the things we need to learn from the mistakes of the past and the poor choices we may have made. The good things we have done in past lives are following us as well. They are manifested in those rewards that seem to come to us from out of nowhere.

I know a woman who received a check from the Internal Revenue Service for thirty two thousand dollars. She had no idea why it was sent to her, she got nervous and called them to find out why she had received the check. The people at the IRS had no idea why she had received the check and told her to just keep it until she heard from them. Five years have passed and she has not heard from them.

It is fascinating to observe the different types of lives we humans can have. There are so many differences in cultures from one country to the next and the customs of each of those countries. The influence of gender in different countries, the role men play and the roles played by women. Our sexual preferences are a major part of the difference in our lives.

The influence of our individual soul-age is huge in how we interpret the events of our lives and life its self. The human experience is so varied and in many ways the same for each of us.

With each new life we can change gender, race and even our sexuality. We will all be heterosexual, bisexual and homosexual in one life or another. Even the time of the year we are born has an influence. Being a Virgo or a Libra will put a twist to a life. It will kind of "tweak" our personalities.

I tend to be a very neat, orderly person. I am a Virgo and this is one of the traits of that sign. The point of the many variables is to alter the experience we have in each new life. What a huge difference there is between being a woman or a man. Being a Chinese person verses a Mexican or a Frenchman.

One of my daughters is a lesbian and it is easy to see the huge difference between our lives. Her life experience is really different from mine, just from how people treat her. Recently I was just reading about 21 people who were sentenced to three years in an Egyptian prison for being homosexuals. This happened in 2003.

Imagine some of the things done to homosexuals hundreds of years ago. Why would there be homosexuals if God did not intend for us to have this be a part of our human experience? Hating a homosexual is just another form of ignorant prejudice.

I have a Caucasian acquaintance who is a younger soul. The things that are said by this individual about other races always set me back. The prejudices that are barely disguised in little jokes about the different races must in some way make people like her feel superior.

Even how a movie is experienced is an example or an illustration of an individual's soul age. Look at how differently each of us reacts to the same movie, some people love it and others hate it. Our soul age is the filter between the events of life and the experiencing of the events by each of us.

FREE CHOICE

Our free choice is what we use to decide our actions when our karma brings an event into our world. Let us go back to being slapped. When that happens, what do we do? Do we strike the person back? Do we walk away? Do we call the police? What choice will we make? The choice we make is going to determine if we stay on the merry-go-around or get off.

If we slap someone back, we have just opened ourselves up to being slapped again. Bad choice! Instead, walk away; this is a good choice, as we create no new karma from this choice. It ends the cycle of experience that would continue for as long as we continue to create the same cause.

The free choice we all have is not really free at all; it too is part of the illusion. When we react to an event rather than respond, we are giving up our free choice. The second we let our instincts take over and we get emotional and are not in control of our actions, we will react and that is dangerous. Anger is then in control and how many good choices are made when we are angry? The only way for us to really use the free choice we have is to be in the moment and respond to the events of our lives. Until we have control of our instincts/lower consciousness we cannot respond, we will only react.

Animals react to events, their instincts kick in and they do what they are programmed to do. If we want to stop reacting as animals, we are going to have to make some changes in how we live our lives every day.

My older sister was killed when she was just forty-three by her husband. She was going to leave him for another man. When she told him, he shot and killed her. He later took his own life. She must have murdered someone in one of her past lives or this would not have happened to her.

We will continue to have the same experience over and over again until we stop the acts which are creating the causes that continue to bring unwanted effects or events into our lives. At some point we have to stop the cycle and move on. Growth is not always swift, but there is always progress. Time is not a factor; we have an eternity to work these things out. We have as many lives as we need to learn. Time is basically part of the illusion.

The best part of understanding this law of karma, for me is understanding that the experiences I did not like are probably my most important and best lessons. The lessons that hurt us the most and are the most painful are going to have the biggest influence on how we think and feel about things and how our moral code develops.

The individual personal growth we obtain is the whole point of having the opposite side of an experience. When you find yourself saying, "I will never be like that" or "I would never do that type of thing to someone," that is the purpose of karma, to help us change our behavioral patterns for the better.

FEAR

Understanding how karma works and influences our lives will make a huge difference in our ability to live life without fear. Fear of things or possible events does not have to be a ruling force in our lives. If fear is ruling your life, then this new understanding of how karma works and impacts your life can assist you in letting go of fear. You can replace the fear mentality with a karma mentality. Fear is a choice.

If something is in our karma, we cannot stop it; it is going to happen. If it is not in our karma, it will never happen. There are *no accidents* in life! Life is not a series of random possibilities and accidents.

I recently visited Lake Arrowhead in the San Bernardino Mountains. Many of the large pine trees are dying from a beetle attack. They were getting quite brown and dry; and the threat of a possible fire was starting to make people nervous. If they were knowledgeable in the law of karma, they would not be afraid.

If those trees are suppose to catch on fire and burn along with all of the other possible effects from a fire, then it will happen. Karma is the deciding factor of this possible event. If it is supposed to happen, then it will. If it is not supposed to, then it will not. Worrying or fear is not going to influence this situation one way or the other.

Not long ago, I had a great deal of money. I felt very secure and quite proud of what I had accomplished with my life. I thought the good times would last forever. I thought my karma would protect me. What I should have known and finally figured out was my karma did bring me exactly what I was going to experience.

Over a five-year span of time, I lost most of my money. It was similar to bleeding to death very slowly. It has been agonizing. The stock market decline, a divorce, plus some bad investments eliminated the wealth that had taken me many years of hard work to attain.

So what was this karma all about? What I have figured out so far from this experience is this: I have set a goal for this life to achieve inner peace. The only way I am ever going to accomplish this is if I have the mental discipline to keep the events of life, just that, events. Then I must learn to be detached from them. This experience is my karma.

The events of life are only events; we decide whether they are good or bad. They are not good or bad unto themselves. They are only good or bad when we designate them good or bad, or when we get a little help from our friends. Our lives are about learning and growing to expand our moral values and to evolve our consciousness.

Trying to figure out what act/cause we did that brought this effect/event into our lives is not important. Our nature is to try to figure everything out. "Why is this happening to me?" Especially the events we do not like.

Try to let go of this way of thinking, as it is a waste of time! Knowing that we are experiencing an event in our lives because of past acts/causes is important. We are never victims! Karma rules!

We must learn to detach ourselves from the events of our life. Money is such a huge part of how we live our lives. The quality of our physical life is based mostly on the amount of money we have. We are taught from an early age how important money is, to use it wisely, save it, take care of it, work hard to get it.

The karma of this loss of money could also be that I took someone's money away from them in a past life and they could not stop me. So now it is my turn to lose money and not be able to control or stop the process.

What greater challenge could the universe present to me to gain the mind control that I must have to achieve inner peace than this event? It has been a wonderful challenge to master my mind and learn to control my thinking while this has been happening. I am not a victim; it is my karma.

There may be other karma involved with this loss of money but I am not sure what it is. It is not important. It does not really matter.

So how can we build a great future? By living righteously every day, one day at a time. We must learn to be in the moment, be aware and control our lower consciousness. The knowledge and understanding of how life works can be put to use to build a wonderful future.

The things we do in this life may not always have a tremendous impact on our current life, but they always will on future ones. We can guarantee a wonderful future by living our lives in this way: "Do unto others, as you would have them do unto you."

The law of karma is in every major religion. It is the law of cause and effect. For the many Christians of the world it is embodied by the idea " You will reap what you sow."

Karma is not about retribution!

I cannot say this enough. Karma is about expanding our moral value system by experiencing the opposite side of an act/cause. All of our kind acts and our not-so-kind acts come back to us. The more kind acts we do, the better our future lives are going to be. Some may even help in this life.

I read about a postal worker who had given over a hundred thousand dollars away to others over the span of about thirty years. He did not make a great deal of money, yet his desire to help other people who were less fortunate than he was drove him to share "his wealth." His kind acts will bring a very pleasant karma to a future life and I would imagine it brought him a great deal of pleasure in this one. He is probably an older soul.

All of the kind and generous acts we perform, both big and small, are going to create our future karma. Most of us perform kind acts every day without even thinking about it. Those little things, like letting someone in front of you when you are on the freeway, will bring good karma into our lives. Being a kind, loving, compassionate human being is the goal of life. Assisting another human that is sad or hurting emotionally is good karma. It does not have to be about money or something tangible. All of the compassionate things we do will come back to us when we are in need. We all need a little love and kindness from time to time.

The whole point of the law of karma is to assist us in achieving this higher level of love and compassion for our fellow humans. We are all brothers and sisters in the family of humanity.

This is why our lives are such a mix of what seems to be good and bad stuff. No one is all bad or all good. We need to understand that we are all part of the same family, no matter what our race, sexual preference, religion, gender, or country of origin.

Our idea of what life is, or is not, is the motivator behind our actions. If every one of us could understand and accept the way the universal laws govern our lives, the planet would be a much different place.

So why can't we? If this all-powerful universal law of cause and effect is taught in every major religion, then why don't we acknowledge it and live our lives differently? It seems like it should be so simple.

Our individual *soul age* is the culprit.

SOUL AGE

We are younger souls or older souls, based on the number of lives we have lived. I like using the comparison to shorter or taller trees. As a short tree/younger soul, we cannot see as far or as wide as the taller trees/older souls. Our ability to understand things is limited. Our ability to comprehend the ramifications of our actions is just not developed enough. Our ability to control our lower consciousness/basic instincts is not developed enough.

As younger souls we are acting instinctually and for the most part, reacting to the events of our lives without thinking first.

Our perception and experience of life is rooted in our soul age. Just stop and think about the many differences in people. If one human has lived 100 lives and another 500 lives, the difference in their total life experiences is huge. The one who has had 500 lives has many more life experiences to draw from. Soul age is a filter between every human being and the events of their lives. It taints all of the events that are part of our experiences. Our individual soul age is what makes each and every event unique to each of us.

Even our sciences have found out that the observer is a part of what is being observed. If a scientist runs an experiment to see if light is a wave, it is a wave. If they run an experiment to see if it is a pulse, then it is a pulse. It is a fact that we see what we look for. We are always part of the experience.

Soul age is the reason one person can read something and think it is good and another person can read the same thing and think it is bad. Soul age is the reason why each of us has such a different experience and bias with just about everything we encounter.

Soul age is the reason one person can experience something and think it is wonderful and another think it is horrible. The positives and negatives of life are subjective. If someone sees or experiences an event in a similar way as we do it is because they are a similar soul age, or they want to be a loyal friend.

We all have a montage of people in our lives who are different soul ages. The younger souls who are a part of our current world are going to bring the richest lessons into our lives. They are going to create the situations that will challenge us the most and require us to grow and learn from the experiences they bring to our life. We will probably not like most of them.

If you have someone in your life who is creating a lot of problems and difficulties, try to step back and take a look at the big picture and examine what is *really* happening. What could you or should you be learning from this experience? What could you possibly gain that will make you a better person in the future? Somewhere in the experience there is a lesson for you. This is your karma in action.

Our world of relatives, acquaintances and friends is made up of older and younger souls. Some people will teach us and some we will teach, we are all here to work on our individual growth and thus the evolution of our consciousness.

If you have children who are younger souls, try to remember they are going to be influenced by everything they are exposed to. If they watch a great deal of television and those shows are filled with violence. Those shows will not create a good impression of how to resolve the differences they will encounter with other people when they are older.

Recently I read in the newspaper about a study that concluded "Violent Television + Children = Violent Children." There is no doubt in my mind that this is true. Young souls are impressionable. The cartoons and video games children interact with today are filled with violence.

An older soul who has lived a number of lives has many life experiences to draw on and thus can perceive the possible ramifications of their actions. They are not acting instinctually, they can control their lower consciousness; they have a great deal of *common sense*. Older souls respond to events; they do not react to them. This is a really big difference in each of us.

When a human can control their lower consciousness and respond to the events of there lives verses reacting to them, they are an older soul. Poor choices are just not part of an older soul's make up. They may not be perfect, but older souls do not make many bad choices.

We are not in control when we react to things. Reacting to things usually results in us being sorry for something we either said or did. Being out of control can happen so quickly. Someone can say or do something that pushes one of our buttons and POW! We lose it and anger takes over.

Many of our poor choices are not intentional; they are out of ignorance and the inability to control our lower consciousness, we are reacting to the events. In many cases we are not evolved enough to know an act is not a good one or we may be out of control and go to the instinctual level of lower consciousness and just react. At that particular moment in time, we just don't care.

Lower consciousness is the monster we are all trying to learn to control and manage. Lower consciousness is behind all of our excesses in life; i.e., food, alcohol, sex, drugs, gambling, work, etc. Does not controlling lower consciousness exempt us from the karma of the acts? No, it is the very reason for karma.

This is why the law of karma is such a perfect law, Karma will teach us what we need to learn to control and thus eliminate our ignorance. The need to be able to control our lower consciousness cannot be emphasized enough. *Controlling the lower consciousness is the key to our happiness.*

As long as we allow our primitive instincts and emotions to rule our actions, we are going to have problems and make poor choices. Controlling the lower consciousness can reduce errors in judgment to a very small number.

Older souls are the teachers of life; they are the humans who try to assist others, like the Jesus Christ's, Buddha's and Gandhi's of the world. They have traveled a long road of many lives and made many mistakes. The old souls are the compassionate Mother Teresa's who share the love and understanding they have built up from having lived many lives.

Older souls have such a different understanding of life. They have made a multitude of mistakes in all of their lives and grown from them. The older souls on the planet respond to events; they do not react. Older souls have the *wisdom, control, compassion, love* and *patience* it takes to live their lives with peace and joy. This wisdom is the essence of their being they call upon to assist and teach the younger souls that are on the planet. They are in control of their lower consciousness.

Basically, everyone is an older soul and a younger soul, as we all have people who are younger and older souls than ourselves. In our own small way we are all teachers. When we reach out to help someone that is having a hard time, we teach. Sometimes teaching can be a simple little hug, a pat on the back, or a kind word.

It does not take much to be a teacher. Showing compassion, listening and understand with love is a huge part of teaching. Assisting a friend when they have asked for help is teaching.

Having an objective perspective to another's p.

helping them come to a good decision, is being a

Not being able to control our anger/basic ins

dangerous. Any number of things can and will happ   ...en we

are out of control. The acts of passion that come from our

personal relationships are in the headlines all the time. When

instincts/anger takes over the craziness begins.

Individual's that are terminated from a job and then go back

and start shooting the people they worked with is a good example

of a young soul that is totally out of control. Someone screaming

and yelling is another example of a young soul that is not in

control of his or her lower consciousness.

We should develop a way of soul age testing. The benefits

from knowing an individual's approximate soul age would be

extremely valuable when it comes to professions like law

enforcement. A young soul in a law enforcement job is a ticking

time bomb. They are going to do something that they should not

do at some point in time; it is only a matter of time.

The Rodney King beating by Los Angles police is a good

example of a few young souls in a situation they were not

equipped to deal with. Their individual prejudices and insecurities

were challenged by the event and they wound up reacting

...vely with aggression like wild animals. Their lower consciousness was in control.

Soul age testing would be no different than the Myers Briggs personality profiling tests. When the tests are used properly they can be of great use to connect the right person with the right profession. The tests would keep people out of the professions that have pressures they are not consciously evolved enough to handle.

Being in the moment is the key to controlling the lower consciousness and thus responding to the events of life. Understanding the law of karma and the influence it has on our lives will also make a big difference.

Karma is a powerful law. The sooner we understand it, how it works and influences our lives, the better. Think of all the wonderful benefits that go with this understanding. It not only gives us the opportunity to reduce the number of unkind things we do, it also allows us to increase the kind acts. The knowledge of karma and how it influences our lives can eliminate living in fear of the infinite possible events of life.

This knowledge can assist us in trying to make better choices and exert more control over our actions. It can assist us in the daily living of our lives in a powerful and positive way. Not because we know good things will come to us as a result of the kind acts we do, but the personal satisfaction of feeling good about ourselves is priceless. It does not matter what one's motivations are; a good act is still a good act. "We get what we give" is so profound a teacher. What a simple yet perfect way for us to learn and grow.

FEAR DOES NOT HAVE TO RULE OUR LIVES.

This is really important. Nothing will ever happen to us in our life that is not supposed to happen. When we embrace the law of karma, we no longer have to worry about getting AIDS or cancer, or being in a fatal car or plane accident. Because nothing will ever happen to us that is not *supposed* to happen in our lives.

We can stop fearing every new illness that pops up in the world, or worrying about something being stolen from us. Anything you can think of that could possibly happen to you; will not happen, unless it is in your individual karma and is suppose to take place.

Living without fear takes a tremendous amount of mental discipline. Our whole society is based on fear. Be careful of this or that. We are bombarded each day by the news that dangers lurk around every corner. We are programmed by the ignorant majority to believe that life is a series of random possibilities/accidents and that one can become a victim at any moment.

The various media's thrive on reporting the horrors of life. Fear is life in America, on this planet, at this time. The news reports run specials on how we can possibly prevent being one kind of a victim or another.

Life does not have to be lived in fear. We have the power to decide what we think about and when we think. We can think about something or not think at all. We can be in a state of non-thinking.

The people in our government use fear to manipulate us to support what they want to do. They tell us partial truths and distort things to prey on our fear of others. They try to get our support for their agendas of what they think is best for us. With the creation of each new law, our freedoms slip away. The few dictate to the many with their crazy actions, as if a new law is actually going to get someone to not do something. It does not work. Laws do not stop people from doing things they should not do.

Fear-based thinking does not have to be a way of life. It can be eliminated!

Fear is an emotion that is perpetuated by a thought.

We have the power through knowledge and understanding to gain control over how we think, what we think and when we think.

Fear can also be instinctive, but I am not talking about that type of fear. I am talking about the fear of possible events. The events that could possibly occur in our lives. Fear of the future. This type of fear is an effect from the cause of unhealthy thinking and the misuse of imagination.

The real power of knowledge is to use it. Karma rules our lives. It is the perfect law; we get back everything we put out. Every major religion teaches this. These religions are not wrong. Karma is simply the law of cause and effect in action. It is absolute, it always works. There are no accidents! There is no good luck or bad luck. There is only karma.

Fear is a very big part of life when we have children. We worry about them getting into any number of situations they are not equipped to handle.

Remember; our children come into this life with their own karma. Nothing will happen to them that is not suppose to happen. If it is in their karma to have a specific experience, no amount of protection is going to keep it from happening. You cannot stop it. You cannot protect your children from their karma.

Everything we want to make happen in our lives will or will not happen within the perimeters of our karma. Suppose you want to change your life in some way. It might be to meet someone to fall in love with. Maybe you want to make more money or have better health. These changes can only happen within the perimeters of our individual karma. If the change is not supposed to be part of this life experience, then we cannot make it happen — no matter what we do.

So what do we do? We all have desires to improve our lives and we all want a better life, no matter how good we have it now. It is good to dream and to want to make our lives better. The key is to learn to accept what our lives are *at this moment* and to understand that with patience and perseverance, change is possible. Patience is the key! Our lives are always in a constant state of change. In America, patience is not very common. We are so into instant results, fast food restaurants, prepackaged food for quick, easy dinners.

INSTANT GRATIFICATION RULES.

We cannot fail if we do not quit. The law of cause and effect is cagey. We can use it in many ways. When we are not getting the results we want, the secret is to continue to make changes to what we are doing/cause, until we get the desired results/effect we are after. Remember; our results will always be within the perimeters of our karma. When we create some action/cause, some effect *must* occur.

This may seem like a contradiction, but it is not. You may want to make a million dollars. If that is not within the perimeters of your karma, it will not happen. However, something will come from the effort to make the million dollars. It might not be exactly what you had in mind; it could be better. If it is not the results you wanted, then the results is only different. We judge everything in life. All of those judgments are what get us into trouble and cause us pain. We will talk about Judgment in more detail, later.

Action/cause will always bring about a result/effect, so doing something to change or improve the quality of our lives *will* result in a change. Once that change has occurred, we have to decide whether it was what we had envisioned or wanted to happen. Again, it might be better.

It could be a long road and take many years to achieve a certain goal or change. The karma involved could be about learning to not be a quitter and to persevere through any number of challenges. If making a lot of money were easy, everyone would do it. Big changes take time, patients and perseverance. To lose weight and maintain a certain level is about a change in eating habits – not for a week or a month, but for a lifetime.

It is like planting a seed and then standing there to watch it grow. You might as well be patient and accept that the change is going to take time to happen. If we do something, something must happen, it is the law of cause and effect. It takes time for things to manifest. Years of working or studying could be what are necessary to get where you want to go. Becoming a doctor or some other professional can take many, many years of work and study to achieve.

YOU CAN NEVER FAIL AT ANYTHING UNLESS YOU QUIT TRYING.

What about feeling empathy for the less fortunate?

Is there room in this understanding of karma to have empathy for the people who are having horrible things happen to them? Does the knowledge of karma change that? It shouldn't. There is a great deal of pain that can come into everyone's life. These events that karma delivers to us, our friends and our family, give us an opportunity to be better human beings.

The knowledge of how karma works will help us to understand why the many events of our lives occur. The same applies to the events that are a part of our families and friends life experiences. It allows us to change the idea that they or we are victims.

We are not victims! No one is ever a victim.

We can still help the ones who need help. We can assist them with love and compassion.

Knowledge is power, if we use it properly. Sometimes we only need to give a friend a shoulder to cry on, to lend an ear or offer a few soothing words.

Have you ever noticed all of the good things that can come from something horrible? Take a big earthquake for example. Big ones can damage property and take many lives. When a large quake occurs, engineers examine the buildings, bridges, etc that are damaged. They then make adjustments to the way they are built in the future. As a result more people will survive the next quake.

Even the horrible death of Nicole Simpson and her friend in Los Angles and the trial of O.J. Simpson brought about a great deal of positive change. The whole event shed light on spousal abuse and how it needs to be treated with a higher priority. It changed the way law enforcement deals with these crimes. It changed the way a lot of people look at these events. People started taking spousal abuse more seriously.

That event was a really big thing. Two human beings brutally killed by knife. If O.J. Simpson did commit that crime, you would not want to be him in future lives. He will be on the receiving side of this same type of horrible event. The karma of his acts will follow him into his other lives and in one of them and probably more than one; he will be on the opposite side of this type of experience. Universal law/karma will show him how much pain the victim experiences when being killed with a knife. It will not be pretty; and he will learn this type of behavior is not enjoyable when he is the one being stabbed, cut and murdered.

Applying the knowledge of karma and how it works to our daily lives takes a tremendous amount of mental discipline. You will not wake up one day and all of a sudden have a change of view on the events in your life and the people around you. This new way of thinking and being will take time to develop.

In America, we are programmed from birth to see things in a totally different way. The common idea is all about "good luck" and "bad luck" and that many accidents can and do happen to each of us, or they are the "God's will." We have developed a routine way of thinking and reacting. Change will only come about when your understanding of this universal law of karma is ingrained in your new way of thinking and being.

It will take time and determination to *reprogram* yourself. It is like putting on a different pair of colored sunglasses to view the world through. Thinking karmically will be a new way of thinking that will change the way you experience life. It will give you a whole new perspective on the events of your life and the people around you and what they are experiencing.

You will be at odds with many of your friends. They all know the world is flat; who are you to say it is round? They will wonder what is wrong with you, why aren't you living in fear? Why aren't you doing things to protect yourself and your family? Are you crazy?

When your understanding of this law is complete, you will eliminate fear as a way of thinking and being. You will know the events going on in your life or the people in your world are only experiencing their karma. You will no longer be a victim, nor will they. You will find yourself accepting things as they are and not how you want or think they should be. You will be able to work through the karma of the moment and gain from the experience. Your individual compassion for others will expand.

You will really appreciate the little things in life more and be thankful for the positive aspects of your life, no matter what they are. You will actually be able to eliminate the whining you may have done from time to time. Your friends and family will love the new you. You will love the new you, and the happy peaceful person you have become will glow and shine.

The only way this change is going to come about is if we learn and develop new habits of thinking. We must learn to control what we think about. We have to reprogram the way we think. We need to learn to "be in the moment" as much of the time as possible.

As our idea of life changes so does the experience of life change. Knowledge changes the idea. In Chapter Four I will share with you the process I have used for many years to make these changes. I am still using them and I still struggle at times myself, even after all of these years. I am not an old soul, I am an *older* soul with many more lives still to live.

CHAPTER TWO:
REINCARNATION

There is no doubt in my mind that we have lived before and we will live again. My basic common sense insists that the idea of one life is ludicrous.

Imagine what a travesty one life would be, if that one life ends at say age six! How crazy is that? There is no way life is a one-time experience.

Reincarnation is the only idea that even begins to explain the enormous differences between each of us humans. Examine the differences of the children in most families, we are not our parents. If life was a one time experience, then we would all come into life with the same moral values, intelligence, view of what life is or is not, etc. Each human would not be as unique as they are. Soul age is the main reason we are so different and why each of us has such a different life experience.

Read up on the subject and you will agree. The most outstanding book I read on the subject of reincarnation was written by a modern day man, Brian Weise. The book was titled, *Many Masters Many Lives*. What a great story this book told. He treated a patient who had a number of mental problems and during the course of her treatment, he learned many things about himself and life. In the beginning he was a man of science and a non-believer. Yet from this experience, he came to embrace the idea of reincarnation.

I believe that our sciences/physics confirm the idea of multiple lives. Everything is energy, energy never ceases to exist. It only changes form. We are spiritual energy beings in a spiritual energy world. We must keep reminding ourselves of this. The human experience is an illusion; it is not what it seems to be. Everything is made up of atoms, and atoms are energy and conscious. Absolutely everything on the planet, and the planet itself, is conscious.

Examine the evolution of the planet. Life progressed as the earth formed. The seas formed and life marched upward from that point. First, funguses appeared. Then plant life, then animals, and then humans. We can review the progress of life forms to see the evolution of consciousness. Each new hierarchy of life form that appeared on the planet was an expression of the evolution of consciousness. Consciousness is what is evolving.

Every new generation of humans is a little smarter, more aware, bolder and more daring than the last. Our consciousness expands just that little bit more, from one generation to the next. Each new generation is able to reach a little higher with the expansion of their consciousness, accomplish more and bring in many new ideas to the human experience.

Our ignorance of what life is and how it works is slowly subsiding. We have less prejudice and hatred, but it is a very slow process. Death is a very important part of the process. Death eliminates old ideas that are not accurate. As our ability to understand life expands, so do our possibilities. The more we become aware of our godliness, the more we progress.

The average soul age of the planet is slowly growing older. As one generation dies off and is replaced by the next, the average soul age of the masses is steadily creeping up.

The real pioneers of human existence are the people who use imagination to make movies. Movies start out as fantasy and the next thing you know; we are actually doing those things. We are accomplishing the things we thought were only fantasy. Our scientists help us reach new heights, as we continue to improve our understanding of what life is and how it works.

It is time for us to close the gap between our technological advances and our spiritual advances. The old superstitions of the past are slowly fading away. Thank God we have death. The changing of ideas and prejudices die slowly enough with it. Change would be nonexistent if death were not a part of life. Without death as a part of life, we would not go forward.

At one time, the Christian religion taught reincarnation as one of its fundamental teachings. It was eliminated when the emperor Constantine agreed to promote Christianity in the Roman Empire. Christianity has gone through many changes over the years, as have all the major religions. The Ecumenical Councils that were held by the leaders of the Christian church brought change, order and consistency to the religion and its teachings.

There are a lot of good books on the subject of reincarnation. Many people can recall past lives and experiences from those lives. Soul age is the difference between us. The number of lives each of us has lived is the totality of our differences as human beings.

The younger souls on the planet have not learned to control their lower consciousness and thus act at a more primitive instinctual level. That is why we have the crimes that one person commits against another. The older souls on the planet are a minority, but they are growing. Life and consciousness on the planet is slowly evolving. Humanity's consciousness is slowly maturing.

The human's who are evolved enough and are awake and aware enough to know they are part of The Play, can do their part to assist those who are not. As the planet and everything on it continues to evolve, life will become less insane. But again, this is a very slow process.

The idea that we might come back as something other than a human being is presented from time to time. Lets go back to the idea that form is an expression of the state of conscious evolution. The essence of form is consciousness; the amount of time this consciousness has existed is the determining factor as to its state of evolution and thus its form. A tree is more evolved than a blade of grass, an insect is more evolved than a tree, a dog is more evolved than an insect, and so on.

Once a human soul has achieved the conscious state of evolution to be a human being they will not regress back to a lower form. The state of evolution their consciousness has achieved will not allow a lower form to form. The vibration rate of the conscious entity that has achieved the human level is too high to create the lower form. We continue to rely on the basic knowledge that everything we see as form is energy, made up of atoms that are conscious. There is only consciousness.

Our higher consciousness forms a body made up of atoms that expresses the state our consciousness has evolved to, so we can have this experience on the planet. Our consciousness has already gone through the lower stages of mineral, vegetation and animal.

There is a great deal of controversy about when the soul or higher consciousness enters the body. Is it when the egg is first fertilized? Is it just before the baby is born? When is this developing entity a human?

It is at the time when the egg is first fertilized. Why? The karma we bring with us starts immediately. If our karma dictates that we are going to have a deformed body, the process must start when the body is being formed, so the deformities can be created while the body is being formed. Our higher consciousness/soul is responsible for the forming of the body.

The one idea I have a great deal of trouble with is the concept of a Devil. An entity that can take over one's body and do evil. Or the idea that evil deeds done by a human are inspired by a force outside of ourselves, in other words, Satan. The evil done by any human is the result of lower consciousness being in control and a young soul; not a devil taking over one's mind and body. The idea of a devil eliminates taking responsibility for one's actions.

Karma, on the other hand, makes us take responsibility for our actions. We are the doers of the deeds. We have to take responsibility for the things we say, do and don't do. The idea presented by the Christian religions – " you will reap what you sow," is in direct contrast with the idea of a devil.

"You reap what you sow" gives responsibility to the individual for all of their actions. The idea of a devil influencing a human to do evil or making them do evil, transfers the responsibility for the humans actions to the devil.

I attended a lecture given by a woman who talked about taking responsibility. The story went something like this. She and her husband were both ill, they had colds and the flu. She was sicker than her husband was, but they had gone to the doctor together. The doctor gave them both prescriptions to get filled. They drove home and after a while, she decided to go to the drugstore to get her prescription filled.

As she was driving to the store she got angry with her husband for not volunteering to go for her, as he was not as sick as she was. She was angry with him for being so inconsiderate. On her way home she realized she had not *asked* him to go for her. When she got home the husband apologized for not going and for not thinking to go.

She told us what an important lesson this taught her about taking responsibility. It was her responsibility to ask him, and only then, if he said no, could she be angry with him.

This is such a great story; it was so profound. We need to take responsibility for our actions or lack of them. Nobody makes us do anything. We make the choices, both good and bad.

I know this couple really well. They got divorced a few years ago. They had been married for a long time. He was not very sensitive to his wife's needs or wants. He was a pretty selfish individual. He was primarily interested in fulfilling his own desires and wants. He was letting his lower consciousness control him.

His wife was an introvert and unable to express her wants and desires. She never said much and when she did, it was not with much force. She was kind of meek and timid most of the time and she did not like any kind of confrontation. She wanted to blame any number of people and things for the demise of the marriage. It was the fault of other people, or of this or that circumstance.

There is no doubt in my mind it was the fault of the two people involved. they did not do the things they needed to do to keep the relationship healthy, such as engage in good communication.

Each of us *must* take responsibility for what occurs in our lives. Not one of our personal relationships will be perfect all of the time. It takes two to make them work and survive over the long term. It is not the responsibility of just one of the people involved. It you have a relationship that is not working; examine it and take responsibility for at least part of what is not the way you would like it to be. Then do something to make a change. The other person is probably unhappy, too.

Taking control of our minds and taking responsibility for our actions is going to bring us closer to the life we all want. The perceived negative karma that comes our way is the result of our past actions, not someone or something outside of our selves.

When we allow our lower consciousness to be in control anything is possible. Listen to the news or read a newspaper. They are filled with stories about young souls who are out of control and functioning in their lower consciousness.

It's like there is a battle of wills to determine which consciousness is going to rule and control our actions. Will we use this lower primitive consciousness that does not understand and does not care about the ramifications of its actions? Or will we use the power of our higher consciousness to control what we do? Will we be in the moment, be aware, be in control and respond to the events of life?

Our higher consciousness has its limits too. How many lives have we lived? How evolved are we? How deep is our understanding of the events of life? How much have we learned from life? How developed are our moral values? How determined are we to control our mind/lower consciousness?

If you are reading this, you are evolved enough to be in a state of awareness that allows you to take responsibility and take control. You would not be interested in this type of information if you were not awake. You are consciously evolved enough to know that we are more than mere humans. If you were at a state of lower conscious evolution, you would not be searching for the answers to life's questions. Being on "the spiritual path" means seeking knowledge.

Remember; we are not some wimpy little human beings subject to the whims of chance. We are Gods. The universal laws govern all humans, the universe and all that is in it. Individually, we can only be as wise as our total lives or soul age. But that wisdom is enough, if we use it.

CHAPTER THREE:
DUAL CONSCIOUSNESS

I have talked about lower and higher consciousness. We are dual conscious beings. It's like there are two of us in this body, and in a sense, there are.

The body is conscious, we are *in* the body. We are the higher consciousness, the soul, the mind. We are the power that gives the body life. We supply the power that makes the heart beat. The body is the lower consciousness, the ego and the personality are facets of it. We have so many different names to call these two forms of consciousness.

The lower consciousness (body consciousness) is the main reason life can get so crazy. Think of the lower consciousness as a totally unruly, ignorant, self-indulgent child, who can be out of control and is only interested in its own gratification. These are our primitive instincts in action. Lower consciousness can never be satisfied, it always wants more to indulge the senses.

That is our lower consciousness; it is very difficult to control. It can be very powerful. It wants to run our lives. Control of this consciousness is especially difficult in our younger years. Once we get past the age of thirty-five, we are functioning more in higher consciousness and thus make better choices and are more in control of the lower consciousness.

Lower consciousness is responsible for all of the mind chatter that goes on in our heads. Haven't you ever wanted to just tell it to "Shut Up!" It is the source of all of the negative thoughts that can take us to some crazy places when teamed-up with imagination.

The lower consciousness is the source of the negative thoughts that are not true about our-selves. It may say, "You are a bad person, ignorant, or incompetent." This lower consciousness can be very brutal to our self-esteem and can make us feel inadequate or unworthy.

When we have a problem with jealousy, it is our lower consciousness and soul age at work again. It is the culprit behind our insecurities and esteem issues. When we are being jealous, we are feeling insecure about whom we are. It has nothing to do with the other person we are feeling jealous over. It is our stuff; it is our incorrect idea about who we are, or our soul age getting in the way of the perfection each human represents.

Lower consciousness will talk us out of doing or trying something even before we give it a chance. Don't listen! Be in the moment and tell it to be quiet! Know that we are gods. We can only fail at something when we quit trying to accomplish it.

I work with my older brother and there are times when he can say something that will push one of my buttons and it sets off my lower consciousness. The lower consciousness is behind the repeating of a thought over and over again in our head, until it makes you want to yell, "Stop!" You know how we can get so emotional about something and then the thought keeps going around and around in our heads. That is our lower consciousness going wild and out of control.

Learning to control the lower consciousness is what we are going to accomplish by being in the moment. Something as simple as taking a *deep breath* can put us back in the moment when the lower consciousness is taking us from the past, to present and then back again. Or taking us into some thought we do not want to experience.

When our lower consciousness is whispering negative ugly thoughts that drive us crazy with worry, turn it off. Switch channels. Do not listen. We do not have to let lower consciousness rule and run our lives when we master being in the moment. Being aware and in the moment gives us the power to switch our minds to another thought. We can control what we think about.

There are two demons for both men and women that go with lower consciousness/the body. For men, it is their aggressive nature and their instinct to procreate the human species. For women it is their emotional and nurturing nature. As with everything these two sides of our basic natures can be both a positive and a negative depending on how they are managed and controlled.

Men need their aggressive trait to succeed in many of their endeavors of business and being the breadwinner, (some women also posses this aggressive trait). If their aggressive nature is not controlled, it will get them into any number of situations that will not be good for them. The newspapers are full of stories about younger souls who were not able to control their lower consciousness and have committed some crime against another human.

Men tend to be the ones who have affairs with other women when married. The woman does not understand it usually has nothing to do with them. The man is indulging his procreative primitive instincts; he is not controlling his lower consciousness, thus letting it rule his actions. An older soul will not have the same difficulty controlling this primitive nature, as a younger soul will.

For women, not controlling the lower consciousness is the anguish that comes from men not being like they are and what they want them to be. Most women are thoughtful and considerate of other humans. Some men are this way, but usually not to the extent of females. Men tend to be a bit insensitive and selfish as far as women are concerned and basically they are.

The basic lower consciousness differences between male and female are huge. Men and women seem to have been created this way to bring these two differences together to create a better whole.

Women tend to see things more from a romantic, emotional, perspective, than men do. My mother always seemed to choose the wrong men for the kind of person she is. When I asked her about this. She responded by saying, she saw men as she wanted them to be, not how they really were.

American society portrays women as youthful, thin, attractive models. These women are used as the benchmark to measure the modern female. When a woman is not of this nature, it is easy for her to feel different, or not normal. This can be very frustrating and hit hard at self-confidence/esteem levels.

Mature women are driven to keep pace with the younger women and have face lifts and any number of other surgeries to appear "normal." There is a lot of pressure to be like the model who is being portrayed as the standard for all to be measured against. This can cause a great deal of stress for women.

Our society does not seem to allow for the normal process of aging and give it the prestige it deserves. The wisdom and beauty that comes with the maturing process is not seen in America as the wonder that it is.

BEING IN THE MOMENT

I have read and heard from different educational tapes that we use less than ten-percent of our mental power. There is no doubt in my mind that this is true. The reason it is true is because we are in the moment less than ten-percent of the time. We make short visits to *now*. We pop in and out of the moment.

How can you tell if you are not in the moment? How many times a day, do you misplace something; i.e., sunglasses, papers you are working with or keys, etc.? When we are in the moment, we are aware of the things we are doing. We are functioning in our higher consciousness and thus operating at our maximum possible power/mental ability.

Have you ever been driving along the freeway and all of a sudden you miss your turnoff or you wonder how you got that far? You were not in the moment.

Any time we are involved in something that takes a great deal of focus and concentration, we are in the moment. Our higher consciousness takes control and we accomplish what we are trying to do.

The lower consciousness is only able to be in control when we are not focused or concentrating and functioning in our higher consciousness. It then seizes the moment to take us on a wild ride to a variety of places.

It is scary how much time we spend connected to past or future events that our lower consciousness has put before us to review. The ideas that come into our minds might be real or just as easily not. So many of the thoughts that pop into our heads are pure fantasy. Our imagination is being used inappropriately.

Lower consciousness teamed up with imagination can be a lethal combination. The lower consciousness is very active with its continuous stream of thoughts. It is like one of those popcorn poppers in movie theaters, spewing out one crazy thought after another, like kernels of popcorn.

We *are* higher consciousness. When we function in the moment, we are functioning in our higher consciousness. We are operating at a much higher level of awareness and mental capability.

Being in the moment is a heightened state of awareness; it is like all of our senses are turned up and are more sensitive. Our hearing is better; the tastes more profound; the sights clearer; and the thoughts more powerful.

Have you noticed that our consciousness works like a flashlight? We really have a rather limited focus and range. We have to direct our consciousness like a beam of light from a flashlight. We direct it to the eyes to see things; to the ears to really listen to the words of a song; to the mouth if we really want to taste something we are eating or drinking. To really experience something, we have to turn/focus our consciousness to the sense that is going to bring us the experience. Otherwise, we experience the thing we are interacting with to a much lesser degree. We are only partially connected to what is going on.

If we cannot solve a problem when we are trying to accomplish something we can turn it over to our higher consciousness. It will find the answer for us –if we are patient. We are a part of universal consciousness. Just present the problem to the higher consciousness before going to sleep at night. Eventually the answer will come to you to solve the problem you are dealing with. The answer will come to you as a kind of *knowing*.

AGING

The fact that we are dual conscious beings is the very reason we age. When we are born, the lower consciousness is dominant and the higher consciousness is subordinate. As we progress through life, the lower consciousness becomes less dominant and the higher consciousness becomes more dominant. As our older, higher consciousness becomes more dominant, our form is showing the progress of this shift of consciousness dominance and thus we look older and seem to be aging.

This shift of conscious dominance is taking place throughout our entire lives. This is why we age. Form is an expression of the state of conscious evolution, of the conscious essence of the form.

The lower consciousness is only interested in the survival of the body. It does everything necessary to assure that it gets everything it needs to survive. As we progress through life, we are functioning more and more as our higher consciousness; we are moving into our higher consciousness, every second we are alive. That is why we seem to get wiser as we get older-- in fact, we are. Our higher consciousness is the sum of all of the lives we have lived. The higher consciousness is the common sense we seem to possess at times. (*A little humor!*)

When we are younger and still dominated by our lower consciousness, we humans do most of the crazy things in life; i.e., commit murders, steal, lie, cheat, assault other people, you name it. The lower consciousness is a thrill seeker and only interested in the gratification of the body. Over-eating, drinking to excess, taking drugs, excessive sex, gambling and a long list of other excesses are a result of the lower consciousness being in control.

To stop these behaviors we have to get control. Being aware and being in the moment will put us in control. We are then functioning as higher consciousness; we are then in control.

The lower consciousness really likes to use the power of our imaginations to concoct any number of possible events that will most likely never happen. If you are in the habit of listening to this craziness, as most of us are. You are probably spending a great deal of your life feeling anxious and stressed about the potential hazards of life.

When one is unaware of the need to be in the moment, we do not know any better, so we listen to the lower consciousness. We worry about everything and anything, especially if we have children. When we add the stimulus from the news about the horrible things that go on in the world to the mix, you really increase stress and worry. Just look at all of the potential dangers that await us.

Fear is a way of life in America. With all of the current things to worry about such as job insecurity, unrest around the world, terrorists and the infinite possible things they could do, it gets even worse. We now have different levels of terrorist alerts. It is like being back in the 1950s, during the early stages of the cold war with all of the things we were afraid *might* happen to us during that era. We were building bomb shelters and stockpiling personal supplies for any number of potential disasters.

But life really never changes. There will always be something to worry about and be afraid of. If living in fear is what you want to do and that is the way you want to live your life, do nothing about being in the moment. You will probably worry yourself into any number of illnesses. Fear and anger are responsible for most of the health problems we have.

The only way to keep the infinite possible events of life, both good and bad, from driving us crazy is with knowledge. Knowledge is power, when we use it. Life is about the choices we make; how we live our lives is a choice. What we think about is a choice.

Understanding the law of karma, how it influences our lives and being in the moment, can save us from living a life full of fear. Knowing how karma works and understanding that it is the Law of Cause and Effect in action, will make our life as enjoyable as it should be.

We are only going to be on the planet for a short period of time. Our visit to the planet is a limited one. Why don't we enjoy every moment of it? Let us savor our lives like some really expensive drink or some wonderful meal. Let us live one moment at a time, one day at a time. That is all we really have anyway.

We seem to easily forget how short our lives are. We are in this incredible, amazing place. We live on this fabulous planet with all of these wonderful things to enjoy. The little things that can and should bring us such joy like flowers, a piece of fruit, trees, a sunset or sunrise, good music, a wonderful meal, a great glass of wine, a hot shower, the beauty of a giraffe, the uniqueness of a porcupine or an elephant. There are so many amazing wonders for us to enjoy. The planet is a virtual paradise.

What a fabulous time to be alive. Humanity has made so many advances through technology to make our lives better and easier. It is so important for each of us to really enjoy just being on the planet no matter what possessions we have. I love thinking of my life as a very short vacation in this amazing place. When we go on a vacation we are happy. We are friendly to others and tend to enjoy all the little things that become special memories. If we encounter problems, somehow they are not as big or as important. How wonderful it would be for each of us to think and live this way every day.

LIFE IS A SHORT VACATION IN THE MOST INCREDIBLE PLACE WE COULD IMAGINE.

When we change our thinking; we change our life one day at a time. Be in the moment; be aware, be in control of what we think.

Christians talk about Heaven and Hell as if they were a place that we go to. I suggest that this earth can be heaven or hell. Look around you at the people who are really strung-out on drugs or have deformed bodies. The ones that are dying from AIDS or have cancer, I bet they would tell you, "This is hell."

Take a trip to the seashore, the desert, or the mountains. Go to a place like Lake Tahoe in California. Take a trip to the Hawaiian Islands or some other tropical paradise, perhaps a rain forest. Could heaven be better? I cannot imagine it could be; especially when you add all of the wonders that are a part of the planet and life.

Everything we could possibly need is provided for us here on the planet. The raw materials to build our automobiles, buildings and any number of other things. The wood and other materials we need for our homes and furniture. The abundance of food like fruits and vegetables. We have fire and rain; it is like the planet has a built in sprinkler system. The snow in our mountains is the water we will need in the summer months.

God/universal mind has thought of everything. We have not even talked about the seas and all that they hold. Why can't this be heaven? (It sure can be hell if we do not take control.) We can make it our heaven, by understanding that our karma will *only* bring the events into our life that we are supposed to have and nothing more. If it is in our karma, we cannot stop it; it is going to be an experience we will have.

If it is not in our karma, it is not going to happen. We must stop living in fear; we need to learn to trust this law.

When an event occurs, try to understand it – then try to accept it and deal with it as best you can. There are normally just a few choices as to what one can do to resolve any given problem. In time, you will be able to *respond* to the events and not react to them.

Thinking in this way is not easy, but we can reprogram ourselves and make it a reality. Practicing being detached is the only way to accomplish these changes. Being detached is the only way to have a happier life. Living life one day at a time is really all there is. These new practices will come through keeping these new ideas in your conscious mind. Do whatever you need to do to accomplish this. For me, it was the use of little notes, stuck everywhere, until this change became a habitual way of thinking.

It is okay for us to cry and feel bad and do a little whining when our life is not going the way we want it to. But remember, you are never a victim! Our karma has given us an opportunity to grow consciously and learn from the experience; that is why we are having it.

Karma will show us the opposite side of some act we have done in the past. Things will get better. Have you ever noticed the cycles our lives go through ups and downs? There are so many events that seem to create the good times and the bad! Each new cycle of events takes us a little higher and somehow our lives are a little better, if you are in a down cycle, be patient; an up cycle is coming.

From my observances, I see our lives as a book. The chapters seem to be about seven years long. It seems like most of the major events and changes occur within a year of each seven-year anniversary, i.e., when we are 14, 21, 35, etc. My life is for the most part in tune with this. I got out of the Navy when I was twenty-one. I was divorced at thirty-four and then again at forty-nine.

I have noticed a significant change in my consciousness awareness at these seven-year intervals. When I turned twenty-eight, it was like all of a sudden I had a deeper understanding of the events of life. I seemed to be able to comprehend things at a deeper level. At age forty-two I had the dream that started me on this spiritual journey and any number of amazing positive things take place, I also became more psychic.

At forty-nine my life blew up and everything changed. I sold my business, got divorced, sold my house, and moved to a new area of Los Angles. The only thing that remained the same was the clothes I owned and some furniture I still had. It was very unnerving because so many things changed at one time. It was like I went through a metamorphosis.

The experience of my forty-ninth year, seventh anniversary was a very negative one. I would be driving along and have to pull over to the side of the road and cry. I went from a thinker to a feeler. All of a sudden, I could feel people's energy and the energy of things. I became more physic. Even my personality profile within Myers Briggs changed.

It actually took me many years to understand who I had become. I was this totally different person. It was an experience like when a woman goes through "the change." I went through a change; it was my conscious dominance shifting. When women experience the change, their bodies are reflecting the change in their consciousness – the shift of conscious dominance. Mind is the cause, the body is effect.

This journey from lower to higher conscious dominance is at times joyful and at times painful. I really like the total difference though. The increased insight and understanding of how life works makes life more enjoyable. I find it is easier and easier to be at peace and to enjoy the state of *just being*. It is like we are becoming these taller trees. Our wisdom and insight into life's experiences is more profound. We have a deeper understanding of the events of our lives and the people in our world.

I find a drive down the coast of San Diego can be so serene, it fills me with a sense of contentment. There is something about being near the ocean or in the mountains that seems to give us a peaceful feeling. As I have aged it has gotten easier to stay detached from the events of life and there is less of an internal battle going on between my lower and my higher consciousness. At times it has seemed like two knights were having a sword fight. Good and evil dueling it out for control of the mind and body.

CHAPTER FOUR:
THINKING KARMICALLY

Learning to think karmically = letting go of fear and replacing fearful thinking with the understanding of how karma works.

Karma is the law of cause and effect in action.

Hopefully, I have explained how the law of karma (cause and effect) works and influences our lives so that you thoroughly understand it. If for any reason you still have doubt that I have explained it correctly. I encourage you to do other reading on the subject. I will supply an extensive list of the many books I have read that gave me the understanding of this law. It will be in the Appendix of this book.

You can also ask God to help you understand this law and how it works. We can all talk to God. God will guide you in your quest to gain peace of mind. Understanding this law will make a tremendous difference in your life. We can eliminate fearful thinking.

The first step into this new way of thinking and seeing the events of life has to start with you accepting the law of Karma as a truth. If this is not a truth for you, you will not adopt this new way thinking and thus change the experience of the many events of life.

There are those events in my life that I still struggle to understand. Be patient with yourself; this is a big change in the way you perceive what is happening in your life. But as I mentioned before, understanding the cause of each and every effect/event is not important. Understanding the law of karma is.

Once you are in the place of understanding that life is a series of karmic events you can begin. The beginning to a new way of thinking and experiencing life should start with some sort of meditation.

MEDITATION

Meditation can take many forms. For example, it can be nothing more than sitting quietly and concentrating, focusing your consciousness on your breathing, an idea or word. It can be taking a yoga class, or it can be doing something that takes intense focus and concentration, like painting a picture, sculpting a piece of art, cooking or gardening, and so on.

Being successful at meditation takes:

PRACTICE—PRACTICE—PRACTICE and
PATIENCE—PATIENCE—PATIENCE.

The reason we need to master meditation is to develop awareness, learn to focus and concentrate. Be in the moment. The lower consciousness loves to wander. Meditating for just fifteen minutes a day, five days a week, is enough to make a positive change. The goal is to be in the moment as much of the time as possible, so we can be *aware* of our thoughts, so we can control what we think about.

Meditation is the ability to concentrate. I have learned that it is possible for a person to be in a state of meditation all day long, by being in the moment. Staying in the moment takes an incredible amount of concentration, focus and mental discipline. The mind wants to wander all of the time. When we are in the moment, we can be aware of what thoughts are in our heads. That awareness will now give us the ability to control what we think about. Without this new awareness we cannot control our thoughts.

Again, the goal of staying in the moment through meditation is to develop awareness. From this we can develop control. It is like choosing which program you will watch on television. We can choose what we think about.

For me, the experience of being in the moment is being able to listen to my thoughts as an observer. I am able to hear the thoughts going on in my head, much like when I listen to a radio or a CD. The continuous stream of thoughts in our heads comes from our lower consciousness. It is a thought machine. The thoughts can be real or made up. The point of being an observer is that we can then control the thought process.

We can change channels and think of something different when there is a thought that we do not like. We change channels all the time when we have music on that is not to our liking. We just switch to something else that we enjoy more, same idea. In other words, we can turn off the static coming from the lower consciousness.

At times, when one is in the moment, thinking stops. The mind is quiet and the normal activity of abundant thought is not in process. We are just being and functioning in our higher consciousness, without the mental visits to the past, the future, or fantasy. With practice, we can both eliminate the flow of thoughts and at times, just *not listen* to the flow of thoughts. To not listen to the thoughts is like standing in a small river and just letting the water flow around you.

When meditating one must let go, trust and relax. Meditation is similar to floating in water, but it is total consciousness we float our consciousness in. The separateness we feel will disappear. We are now at one with total consciousness. This is why meditation can give us such a feeling of peace.

If we do not focus our consciousness onto a thought and go with it, it will just go away, like smoke in the wind. By not directing one's consciousness on a thought, it disappears and is usually replaced by another. It is a never-ending process.

This ability to stay in the moment is critical. It is not something you will master in a day, a week or a year. It will take years and years to gradually build your ability to be in the moment. We are trying to gain control over the mind. To do so, you will have to be very patient and determined.

I have spent the last fifteen years working on this concept and believe I am in the moment only about seventy five to eighty percent of the time. But believe me, it is worth the effort. Every second you are in the moment is to be cherished. It is like a visit to heaven.

I wished I had written the dates down when I was in the moment for three consecutive weeks. They were the most incredible, amazing, blissful three weeks of my life. Words cannot describe the state of peace that accompanies this prolonged visit to *now*. The Buddhists call it Nirvana.

Being in the moment is being connected to God/total consciousness. You feel like you are floating several inches off of the ground. Joy seems to ooze out of every one of your pores. Everything is heightened when we are in the moment; everything our senses bring to us is more intense. The colors are richer, the tastes are tastier and the feelings more intense. Absolutely everything is enriched and heightened.

You are going to really enjoy the visits to now, especially when they are prolonged. The peace you have longed for will be yours. We all share one common goal in life: to be happy. Mastering being in the moment will bring you the happiness you have wanted for your entire life.

When we are in the moment, we are able to feel the connection to the other life on the planet. We are able to feel our connection to God. When we are in the moment the simple act of walking on the beach, or a hike in the mountains, will give a person the feeling of being at one with the universe.

All is consciousness; everyone and everything is consciousness. Everything that appears as form is part of the same family of consciousness.

When you really think about time, there is only now – this very moment. The past is only a now that has gone by; the future is a now that has yet to be. We really only ever have this moment of now; it is a constant now that we live in.

When we are in the moment we are aware of our thoughts and thus can exert control over what we think about. Imagine the power of this concept. We *can* control what we think about. Why would you want to think about something that brings you pain, or makes you unhappy?

What is to be gained from dwelling on some past experience that we perceive as a negative? Notice I said "perceived negative." Life is subjective, and each of us decides what is good, or bad and what we like or do not like. The past events that litter all of our lives cannot be changed. They are behind us; we have to learn to let them go. Being in the moment is one way to do that. The past events occurred for a reason. That reason was to teach us, to show us the other side of an act. The event was meant to be a learning experience. It was our karma.

Almost all of our emotions come from our thoughts; our emotions are the body reacting to a thought, the cause is thought, the effect is emotion. Women can experience emotions from the physiological changes that occur from being a female – their body cycles. Chemical imbalances in our bodies can also bring unwanted emotions. Most of the time, if our thoughts are controlled our emotions are controlled.

What can we do to develop the habit of staying focused and in the moment? We have to make a conscious effort. I've found little notes really help me to do that. I put them on the dashboard of my car, on my computer at work and around my house. If you want to develop new habits, you have to make a concentrated, conscious effort. It requires you to *do* something. My notes will be short statements like "Be in the moment," "Think now," "Think spiritually," "Trust," "Focus," etc. Use any method or note that works for you to help you stay in the moment and keep that idea in the forefront.

To make a change we must keep the new idea conscious. We have to make a conscious effort to stay in the moment. This is not something you will just remember to do.

Simply taking a deep breath can bring you back into the moment. It stops the thinking process for just a second, which is long enough to get you back in the moment.

I found that being around other people who are interested in the spiritual aspect of life helps me. Talking with them makes it easier for me to stay on the spiritual path and keep focused. Positive, happy people are easier to associate with and are more uplifting. It is easier to be in a positive, happy state of mind.

We see what we look for is not a clever cliché. It is a fact. When we hear the statement, "the glass is half full," or "it is half empty," it is our way of looking at things. Keeping a positive perspective takes an *effort*. It is not going to just happen. Staying in the moment is the key to keeping a positive perspective about life and it is worth the effort.

Just think, we can now control what we think about. This is so profound! This is so powerful!

When we perceive an event or something as a negative, what we are saying is this is not what we wanted to happen. It is not what we want to be a part of our lives. It is outside of our idea of what should be.

That rascal karma bringing events into our lives that we would rather not have.

Life is an idea. When we change the idea, we change the experience.

Judgment of the events of life is the source of most of our problems. Why do the Buddhists tell us to "be detached?" Because putting space between an event and ourselves allows us to really examine and experience the event without emotion – as an event. Every event in life is just that, an event. In short, something for us to experience and embrace. We choose to like it or not like it. The events of life are always subjective.

Isn't it much easier to give a friend advice on something going on in their life, than to work through one of our own problems? This is because we are detached from the problem. It is not our problem. It's their problem, so we can be more objective. We can be detached and clear-headed about choosing the best solution. We are able to see the choices and weigh them to find the best available solution and which may be the better choice to make.

I find that most of the situations that come up in my life involve making a choice from a few possibilities to deal with what needs to be dealt with. So I choose and go on, sometimes with a bit of whining or a curse and mumble under my breath. But I then let it go and move on. Progress can be slow at times, but with determination, there will be progress.

Dragging all of the past "stuff" of life around is just too much work. It gets too heavy. Learn to let things go! Lighten your load. Find a way. It can be done if you really want to let go. It was your karma.

So you did not have a great childhood and you've now reached the age of forty. It's time to move on. It was your karma. What did you learn from that childhood experience? Did it make you been a better parent? Did the negative experience help you to become a better person? What did you gain or learn from it all? Learning was the point of experiencing the event. What did you gain and how did you grow from the experience that you did not like? Was there behavior you will probably not repeat in the future? Has the experience helped you to make behavioral changes?

By focusing on the positives gained from an experience, it is easier to let go of the things of the past. Somewhere in the experience, there was a positive. Try to find it. Know it was your karma. Use the knowledge of karma to eliminate the victim mentality and let the experience go.

So many people have bad marriages and they spend the remainder of their lives agonizing over the experience. My mother has done this. My father left her with four kids and provided no financial support to-boot. She has never gotten over it, even after fifty years. It was her karma, she did this type of thing in a past life and now it was her turn to be on the receiving side of this type of experience.

Suppose, in a prior life, you were an abusive parent to your children? In this life your karma would put you in the place of the child who was being mistreated. From that experience, you would learn that it is not much fun being the abused person.

I dated a woman who experienced this in a once-removed way. Her father was very abusive to her brother, but not to her. Her karma was not to be the child being abused, but she was part of this family. She still learned a lot from her place in this environment. She most likely already had her turn at being the abused child in a previous life. She was not an abusive parent in this life; she has learned it is not fun to be abused.

Sometimes taking some action will assist you in letting go of an experience that was part of your past that you just cannot let go of. I had a problem letting go of a particular event, so one night I decided enough was enough.

I took a coffee cup from my cupboard that I did not need, and I embodied this cup with what I wanted to be rid of. The coffee cup would symbolize the thing or event that I wanted to eliminate from my life. I opened the door to my back yard to the cement patio. And I threw the cup down onto the concrete with the idea that when it broke, the old event would no longer be a part of me. I was destroying the myth of this idea, and ridding my life of the residue.

It was such an exuberant feeling. But the cup bounced up from the cement patio and ricocheted off of the building next door. Then it knocked the wind chimes out of a tree in the backyard, creating a tremendous amount of noise as the chimes hit the patio floor. It was so funny to see how this act had escalated to be something quite spectacular.

The symbolism of doing something like that can be helpful to rid yourself of some old stuff that just won't go away. Being in the moment will also assist you in letting those old wounds heal. When the negative thought arises, switch to something else. You can learn to just turn them off, like a television show you're tired of watching. Just stop watching this program and eventually it will stop coming on.

You could just as easily take some balloons and fill them with helium to make them float away. Then take a marker and write what you want to let go of on the balloons. Then one by one, let them float up into the sky and declare an end to dragging this *stuff* with you through life. Couple this with the power of being in the moment and the ability to choose what you think about and you have a powerful program.

The work to be in the moment should become a way of life – a routine part of our daily existence. It should be something you just do. One of the things we all do every day is to eat. Think of this as a new aspect of our diet. Many people are now interested in eating healthier food. This is *real* health food. We are going to grow old anyway; we are going from one day to the next anyway. Why not put out just a little effort to be in the moment each day as a part of the way we live, to improve the quality of our lives?

Being in the moment will make a bigger difference than a new car, or a new outfit. *Things* have such a limited impact on our lives. All of a sudden that new car that brought you so much pleasure is a couple of years old. We can never satisfy the senses of our lower consciousness.

Being in the moment takes no more effort than maintaining your weight at a desirable level. It is a mental discipline supported by a few physical disciplines. Being in the moment will bring a lifetime of joy.

I have set a personal goal for this lifetime. To realize inner peace and thus be in a constant state of peace, no matter what events are going on in my life.

So what if I do not get there in this lifetime? Whatever progress I make in this lifetime will carry over into my future lives and put me that much closer to my goal in my next life.

Just imagine how wonderful our life will be if we are able to accept the events of life without judgment. We can do it! It is not a fantasy! It will just take patience, time and effort to get there mentally. We just have to change the way we think about things. Our ideas about what the truths of life are is what shapes our experiences of life. We can reprogram our minds with new knowledge. Being on the spiritual path is the pursuit of knowledge.

When I studied Buddhism, there was a great deal of talk about being in a state of Nirvana. After a great deal of reading, I understood this to be a mental state of peace, bliss. These people were in a constant state of now. Experiencing Nirvana is being at one with God/higher consciousness.

With the input of additional information, I have come to the conclusion that this instant state of Nirvana that was being realized by people had probably taken them many, many lifetimes to achieve. It is like the overnight success that takes ten years to achieve. I am sure that a number of famous people will tell you, their overnight success came after many years of hard work and practice.

When we get control of our minds, we do not have to live in fear, be angry or live with anxiety and pain.

Let's start now! Live without fear. Understand the law of karma rules our lives. Be aware – be in the moment.

We do not have to fear the unknown. If it is in our karma, we can't stop it; the experience is going to take place. If it is not in our karma, it will never happen. Using the knowledge of this law to set you free from fear. With patience, we can learn to wait and see what our karma will bring us? Then deal with it. How much time do you spend worrying about the many things that *might* occur in your life that never do? It is a waste of our imagination and power.

But shouldn't we take precautions? Yes and no. I have no desire to run across the freeway when traffic is moving at full speed to see if my karma would keep me from being killed or not. That would really be stupid in my mind.

I cannot stop the things that are in my karma from finding me. They will.

I do not need to worry when I step on to an airplane. If it is suppose to crash and it is my time to die, then I am *supposed* to be on the plane.

I will never have an experience that I am not supposed to have. There are no accidents in our lives!

We are like an incredibly powerful computer, but without a manual to explain how to use it. Understanding who we are, how we work and the laws that govern us, is the key to peace and happiness. We can rise above primitive instinctive thinking and reactions to events.

We can control what we think about, and how we think. Being in the moment gives us the power to decide the thoughts we have and allow to be a part of our world.

CHAPTER FIVE:
GOD

One idea that really helped me to change my understanding of life was what God is – or is not. It was another powerful idea behind the elimination of fearful thinking.

God is an idea.

How did this idea get to where it is today? Did early humans just know there was some kind of higher being? Did they know someone or something just had to have created this world and all of the wonders that abound in it?

Humans, at one time, thought there were multiple gods. One for the many different aspects of the human experience. At one time, we were also sure the earth was flat.

As our human consciousness has evolved, we have become more aware. Our collective human consciousness is rising with each new generation. We just know things that we did not know before; we can feel and sense more. We can see from looking at the earth and how it works, that all of this is not by accident. This planet and the way it functions is by design.

Jesus Christ told the world thousands of years ago, "we are the children of God." I truly believe this to be a fact. It is like we have three parents, our parents gave us our body, and our consciousness comes from God.

God is total consciousness.

That is what my studying has taught me. There is only consciousness. Nothing but consciousness exists. All atoms are conscious; the smallest particles that make up an atom are conscious. Atoms are not things; they are consciousness in motion. There is nothing other than consciousness.

Consciousness is the essence of all that is. It expresses itself as energy/atoms. Atoms are the fiber of all that appears to exist. Consciousness is the essence of the various states of evolution. The human ability to imagine or fantasize and then create are some of its many facets. It is the essence of the thought process and reasoning, plus the human ability to know one's self. It is the ability to connect various possibilities. All of the various aspects of the mental, intellectual and emotional processes are but different facets of it. Nothing but consciousness exists. Everything that exists is but a reflection of it's many sides.

All form is an illusion. The Buddhists teach this idea. It took me over three years just to understand what that one simple statement meant. "Life is an illusion." It was not until I read a book about how our senses work that I understood what that meant. If our senses did not work the way they do, this experience we are having would not seem to be – as it seems to be. It is our senses that delude us into thinking life is real and permanent, that things are soft or hard, hot or cold. Instead, everything is energy. Everything is made up of atoms.

Our senses pick up vibrations from everything. Everything is pure energy, and energy vibrates. The vibrations we receive via our senses are converted into an electrical signal that goes to the brain and forms a mental picture from the vibration. The brain is not the mind. The brain is a powerful device that allows us (higher consciousness) to experience this reality.

Form demonstrates the current state of evolution of the conscious essence of the form. The essence of all form is the soul of that form, the very heart of its existence, which is consciousness.

We are not the body, we are only *in* the body. The body only defines and demonstrates that our consciousness has evolved to the advanced state it has. The body is lower consciousness.

Every form – a tree, a dog, a blade of grass, is conscious. The form illustrates the state of evolution the conscious essence has achieved up to this point of its evolution. Everything is either more or less consciously evolved. The hierarchy of form is the expression of the evolution of the consciousness that is its essence.

My understanding of what God is goes something like this. Think of God as an extremely large *ocean,* as though the total universe is this ocean. Everything that exists is a drop in this ocean. These drops are what make the ocean an ocean. All of the universe and everything that is, is a part of total consciousness, i.e., God.

God is total consciousness! We are a part of God; we are the children of God! We are Gods! We are God beings.

That is why so many teachers and philosophers talk about the connectedness of things. Everything is connected, as everything is a conscious drop in the ocean of total consciousness.

This understanding of God has helped me so much. Whenever my lower consciousness spews out negative thoughts and I feel like a wimpy human, I relate to what I just said in this way. I have developed a series of statements that bring me into the moment and center me with a feeling of peace and power. They go like this:

"I am of God!" " I am a God!" "I am at one with God!"

When I make these statements, they bring me into the moment. I am then centered and in a state of peace and power. It is like watching television; you can control the channel, so why not watch something enjoyable?

I like to end these statements with, "I am at one with God." I kind of hold that thought for a while. It makes a connection that gives me a feeling of oneness with God. This oneness is real; we are at one with God and we are a part of God. We can communicate with God; we are Gods, all of us.

This is a universal truth!

This is what God is.

This is not my truth, but a universal truth. Investigate it yourself. You will find out, as I did, it is a fact! Jesus Christ was right. We are the children of God.

The only thing that exists is energy, consciousness.

Jesus was correct when he taught, " We are the children of God," not in some hypothetical sense, but actually.

We are not some poor, inept little beings who are here to endure all of the potential hazards and accidents that can occur in life. Life is not random and accidental. It is purposeful, with order and laws.

If you think about life, there are only three possible choices. Life is either a series of random possibilities. Life is purposeful and is governed by laws. Or life is a combination of the two. I am convinced it is governed by laws and is purposeful, our scientific investigations have revealed the truth of this.

It would be impossible for this planet to work the way it does, with its harmony, synchronicity, and connectedness, for it all to be the result of random possibilities. The way our planet's systems work would have required way too many random possibilities to be in harmony, to get to where we are today. The way the planet works is by design!

We only need to understand what the laws are and how they work. We can control our future, one day at a time. We build our future one day at a time. When we can master *responding* to the events in life, rather than reacting to them, we will be in control and much happier.

How can we be in control? Be in the moment, be aware, control what we think about? Control what we do? This sounds simple, but is not easy.

We have to reprogram ourselves. We have to make a conscious effort every day. We have to *do something* to make the way we think and act different every day. We need to learn to take life one moment at a time, one day at a time.

Start today! Why wait? Why be unhappy? Why be miserable? Why be out of control?

Life does not have to be lived as a knee-jerk reaction to the events of life. We can live peaceful, happy lives. Life is about choice. We can make this choice.

Does it seem like there should be more to God than this? What about this kind, loving, sometimes angry god? What about the God who gives to some and punishes others; what about that God? He, or she, does not exist. It is a great story that has been told to us for a long time. God does not micro-manage we humans or the universe.

God is so amazing and profound. Just look at the universe, this planet and all of the little things that make it the perfect place that it is. Try to imagine life without fire, water, rain, snow, or the sun. The relationship and connection of things to each other is so amazing. What an incredible consciousness that put all of this together to make the earth as it is. The universe as it is – so vast and plentiful.

You just know there is other life on other planets in the universe. Probably not in our form, with our senses, but other conscious, intelligent beings have got to exist. It would be absurd to think we are the only intelligence in the whole universe.

I think another great use of this understanding of our relationship to God will really help the many people who have low self-esteem. It seems that quite a few women have low self-esteem. I know this is not limited to women, because men have this problem, too. It just seems like this is more of an issue for many women.

Low self-esteem is our lower consciousness at work again. It is the culprit behind this incorrect idea of ourselves. Lower consciousness is the voice that whispers those negative words to us, that tries to make us feel unworthy, stupid, or ugly. Lower consciousness is behind the negatives we get in our heads that do not belong there.

Being in the moment and replacing that negative crap from the lower consciousness with the truth is another reason to make being *aware* a way of life. We are the children of God. We are Gods! Switch to this idea when a negative thought about who you are makes its way into your head, and change the channel.

We are incredible, amazing human beings capable of doing fantastic things. We do not have to be rocket scientists to believe in our Godliness. The simple little things each of us is capable of doing are what make it so.

Just look at what we humans have accomplished and created so far. By using the various substances that are on the planet, we have made everything that we need and more to live well. Look at the evolution of our accomplishments, consciousness is what is evolving and that is why we are able to continue to progress and create these new tools to make our lives easier and better.

The fact that we can now go into space is a good example of how our consciousness is evolving. We are achieving far greater things than ever before in man's history. We are gods and only limited by our own imaginations.

The creative things we all can do, is an expression of our godly status. Every, human, is creative in their own way. Whether it is being a good cook, or being able to sew a dress, or paint a picture. There are thousands of ways we express our individual, godly, creative powers.

It is so easy for us to take even the simple things we humans can accomplish for granted. Can any animal put a piece of thread through a needle? Can any animal create the thread or needle in the first place?

Low self-esteem comes from the ignorance of our soul age and not relating to our godliness. We are listening to our lower consciousness. Our soul age is a block that gets in the way of us knowing and understanding this truth. If we are not consciously evolved enough, this cannot be our truth. The old traditions and superstitions about who we humans really are die slowly.

The negatives our lower consciousness spews out must be controlled. This unruly monster cannot be allowed to run our lives, or ruin our lives. Being in the moment takes the control out of lower consciousness hands and puts it where it belongs – in ours, the higher consciousness. We *are* higher conscious beings! We *are* Gods!

When we control what we think about, we are going to make this one terrific life. The peace we will experience alone makes the time spent reprogramming ourselves and gaining mind control, a goal we should all strive to accomplish.

Functioning in our higher consciousness will bring us to our highest possible levels of achievement. Imagine being happy and content with just being on the planet and enjoying all of the wonders that are here for us. What more should we really want?

We all desire to live well, have good health, food for the table, a roof over our heads and some of the other things that we are told will make us happy. But when the *things* of life take over and become our primary reason for living, we have gone too far. We need to step back and do a reality check.

One of the things that I have observed is the contentment with life that many Hispanic people seem to have. They do not seem to tie their happiness to their possessions. They get enjoyment from family, cultural traditions and a good meal. They like getting together to celebrate the wonderful customs that go with their heritage and religious beliefs. I know not all Hispanic people are of this mindset; it seems they might have older souls among them.

ANGER

Anger is an emotional experience, originating from thoughts or primitive instincts of our lower consciousness.

It is an effect from a cause. Anger is an emotion that can be eliminated from the human experience by controlling the lower consciousness and thereby, the emotions.

Control over one's anger is another product of being in the moment. Anger is the result of *reacting* to an event rather than responding. Responding to an event will give you the control to not do the things you will be sorry for later. Being in the moment allows us to control anger.

Our primitive instincts are a part of the basic makeup of our lower consciousness. They are part of the survival mechanisms of our lower consciousness/body. The only way to gain control over lower consciousness is by being in the moment consciously.

Have you ever noticed the biggest loser, when anger takes control, is the person who is angry? They are the one who is upset and getting their stuff all over other people. They usually make an ass out of themselves by doing or saying something they would not normally do or say.

Uncontrolled anger is what creates many illnesses. The energy from the anger goes to different parts of our bodies and causes us to be ill. It disrupts the peace and harmony of our being. It disrupts our Chi (internal energy flow).

Anger does not have to be part of ones life experience. By being in the moment, we are aware, we control the mind. We can think the thoughts we want to think. We can *respond* to events! We can stop acting like primitive animals.

Anger is a result of the lower consciousness controlling our actions. Our lower consciousness is the source of the idea to retaliate against someone for something we think they did to us, that we did not like. Men are especially vulnerable to anger ruling their lives. Men have aggressive primitive instincts that are part of the male body's basic makeup. We have to learn to control these primitive instincts. These instincts can take us to a state of out-of-control very quickly and easily.

Just examine the prison populations. What is the majority of the population? Men! Who starts the wars? Men! The male aggressive instincts are a monster that needs to be controlled. It is harder for some males and much easier for others to control their instincts. Individual soul age is what makes the difference in each human's ability to control these instincts.

Our lower consciousness is the source of all of our negative thoughts and actions. Negative thoughts are what get us into trouble, make us feel bad and cause us all kinds of grief when they are not controlled. We tend to just react to things without stopping to think and use our higher consciousness.

It is our lower consciousness that stops us from doing something before we ever start. It is the source behind "be careful you might fail" before we begin some new endeavor. Being in the moment will put us in control and we will be functioning in our higher consciousness.

Think of the lower consciousness as this undisciplined, self indulgent, ignorant being that is only interested in its own gratification. It is like a very spoiled child that always wants its own way. It is the primitive, instinctive side of our being. It can also be evil, our own individual Devil.

Six years after getting divorced, I am still finalizing some of the financial aspects from my second marriage. The emotions from this experience have been incredible. My lower consciousness has had me going from one extreme to another. The thoughts that come from this lower consciousness can be scary. Anger and resentment have tried to take control of me on many occasions. I feel like I am wrestling a giant bear at times. Have you ever had this experience?

We can slay this dragon – lower consciousness – with the control that comes from being in the moment. We can keep it from running and ruining our lives. We just have to step back and put our "karma glasses" on and look at what is going on from the bigger picture. It may take time to master this way of thinking on your own. Having a friend who is already on the path can assist us. They will be the one who is detached from the problem and can remind us to really examine the circumstances of what is taking place. It is our karma that is bringing us something new to experience. Some new challenge for us to grow and learn from.

I have a friend who is serving a ten-year prison sentence for rape. You would not believe this person could have done something like this. What was he thinking?

Years ago he worked for me as a production manager when I was running a printing plant. He was married and had two very nice children. He had been in the Marines and served his country with honor.

We parted ways when I went into sales and he stayed in production. But we worked for the same company, so I heard about him from time to time. He later got divorced and was single for a while. When he remarried a few years later, it was to a much younger woman. The marriage did not last for many years and then he was divorced again, living by himself.

He was angry about many things in his life. This anger made him just a bit crazy. The next thing I heard he had been arrested for luring a young woman to his apartment and then taking her out in the hills and raping her. Thankfully, he did not kill her.

His lower consciousness was obviously in control of his actions. He could not do something like this and be functioning in his higher consciousness.

The lower consciousness will be in control, if we do not take control by being in the moment. Anger and fear will rule our lives and make this life an ugly experience. We will do things we should not do and will be sorry for later.

A lifetime is a very short experience. Controlling our thinking by being in the moment is the only way to make it truly enjoyable. We are then functioning as higher consciousness. The positive change to the experience of life is profound when we functioning in our higher consciousness.

CHAPTER SIX:
JUDGMENT

Judgment is a way of life.

We judge everything from objects that are hot or cold to things that taste sweet or sour. We naturally judge things and most of the judgment is at the lower consciousness level. The lower consciousness judges as a way of providing for the needs of the body. We can learn to discern the difference between this type of judgment and the judgment of others, ourselves and the events of life. Judgment of others and the events of our lives can be controlled and *should* be controlled, to achieve a higher level of happiness.

When we are in control of the judgment of others and life in general we are saving ourselves a great deal of anxiety. Most of our judgments result in our own anxiety and the anxiety of others. Judgment of others is a waste of time and energy; it serves no purpose other than perhaps to make us feel superior. I am always of the idea that I have enough to do to take care of myself. I cannot live other people's lives and I certainly cannot change anyone.

Avoiding the judgment of others seems like a simple choice, but it is not, since old habits are hard to change. It takes awareness and a mental effort to alter our old ways of thinking and being. But it is certainly worth it.

I have wrestled with myself on the issue of judgment for quite a while. I know from personal experience, this way of thinking is not easy to change. It takes determination and the desire of a better, happier, more peaceful life to make the change. The benefit of eliminating judgment is a more contented happier life.

One change I decided to adopt several years ago, that has been a good choice was to not put people in a position where they have to possibly pass judgment on what I say or do. When someone asks me to do something, or to go someplace with them and I did not want to, or cannot for some reason. I simply tell them, "thank you, but I cannot." I do not include a reason or excuse in the answer.

When we do not give someone an excuse or reason about why we do not or cannot do something. Then they do not have to decide if it was a good enough reason or not. It is like saving a relative from suffering from a case of amnesia by not lending them money. (*More humor!*)

Judging the events of our lives seems to be normal human behavior. But is it normal behavior and is it a good way to behave? I suggest it is not, and that it can be eliminated from the way we live our lives.

Why should we make this effort to change this type of behavior? Because we are only on the planet for a short period of time and we should make it as enjoyable as possible. When we cease to judge, we are happier. Think about the positive side of this behavior change. We will be happier! Why will we be happier? When we eliminate the judgment of events, we save ourselves the pain that can go with the judgment.

The events are only events, that is all. They are neither good nor bad in themselves, but only as we decide them to be good or bad. The events of our life are our karma presenting us with opportunities to grow. Our life events are there so we can experience the other side of a cause we initiated at an earlier time in our existence.

The events are good when we feel they add something to our lives or bring something positive to our lives. Events are bad when we think they bring a negative to our lives. The good and bad of our lives is subjective. We seek acceptance of our position by discussing these events with our friends and family in order to get their confirmation. "Yes, that was terrible; I would feel bad too!" Or "yes this is great, I hope something like that happens to me."

They have to agree with us, if they love and care about us. We would be very angry with them if they did not. Since the people we rope into this type of discussion are our family or friends, it is their duty to agree with our point of view.

DETACHMENT

The key to living a life of non-judgment needs to have detachment in it. We cannot cease to judge if we cannot detach from the events that occur in our lives. Non-judgment is going to take a great deal of objectivity and that can only happen if we can master being detached.

These changes can only happen when we are in the moment, aware of our thoughts and controlling them. This can happen when we accept and understand that karma rules the events of our daily lives. We need to establish a foundation in our way of thinking, that we will only experience the events we are suppose to experience and no other.

Karma rules! Life is *not* a series of random possibilities or accidents.

Being detached is like being in a theater watching what is taking place up on the stage. When we are in the audience watching, we are detached. When we are emotionally involved and are up on the stage being a part of the play, it is extremely difficult to remain detached. When we are on the stage we cannot be objective and will probably *react* to the events, rather than respond. When we respond to events it is with much more control and purpose. The results are going to be better and in the long run, more positive.

The ability to control our lives and be happier and more peaceful all comes back to our ability to be in the moment, be aware and to take control of what we think about.

What about the joys of life you say? Will we become unfeeling robots with all of this control? When we give up the judgment of events and are detached, we do give up the short-term joy of the moment and replace it with a long-term peace, contentment and bliss. The bliss that accompanies accepting what is and knowing the events of our life is our karma in action.

Isn't almost every individual act we engage in done with the intention of bringing us happiness? Is this new way of thinking and being too much of a fantasy? Not if we can get to where we manage and control our thoughts. Be in the moment, be aware and control what we think about.

We *can* do it, by practicing being in the moment all day long, every day. We just have to make it a way of life, the way we live from day-to-day. This is a lifetime behavior change. A change in the way we think and act.

Some days we will only progress a small amount and other days it's like we have conquered the world. Some days it will feel like you have gone backwards, be patient, you will persevere.

The Buddhists say, " A journey of a thousand miles begins with a single step." So let's take a step each day we arise to greet the new day. Let us make being in the moment a new way of living and being.

To make these changes it takes:

PATIENCE—PATIENCE—PATIENCE!

PRACTICE—PRACTICE—PRACTICE!

Try not to get caught up in whether you are making progress or not. Do not judge your progress or lack of it. That judgment thing again, it influences so many things in our lives. Just know, you will progress! We have to progress when we are doing something; i.e., it is the law.

Practice everyday to be in the moment. We should choose the things that we think about with the same care we give to the food we eat, or which medical facility we go to, or whom we marry. Aren't all of those choices meant to improve our lives and make us happy? How much joy do you get from thinking about something negative? Probably not very much.

So why do it? You don't have to!

The effort to be in the moment will become a way of life and in time, a habit – something that we do automatically every day. But we have to make being in the moment a daily, conscious effort.

Do whatever works for you to keep being in the moment conscious. (I like the notes.) It takes twenty-one days to develop a new habit but if we make this a permanent behavior change, a new way of living. A new way of being. After a while, you will just do it every day. You will *be* this new person.

Can you see all of the benefits from staying in the moment? They are so huge! Progress is slow and not so steady, so one must be focused and determined. Practice everyday as a way of living and being. I am amazed at how each day adds up. The up days, when we are doing really well, are like... "Yes!"

Sometimes it will take me a couple of days to realize that I have not been being in the moment. Once that happens, I regroup and start fresh. Sometimes our friends or family can help us realize we have not been doing well. It does not matter who or what makes us realize we are off track. What ever assists us in getting back on track is all that is important. Being stressed or anxious is always a good sign you are off track and are not in the moment.

I can tell that I am not being in the moment when I have gotten caught up in some hypothetical idea about what should be or I am concerned about something that may happen. I then get back on track with even more focus and determination.

The key is to not give up. There will be times when we will only have one really good day in a month, but that one day will be one *great* day. Then we will have two days, and then three.

Don't quit and don't judge whether you are making progress or not. We can only fail at something when we quit trying. This is a total life behavior change we are after, and any progress we make will follow us into our future lives.

CHAPTER SEVEN:
APPRECIATION OF LIFE

WE ARE ALL GOING TO DIE, i.e., LEAVE THE BODY.

We just don't know when.

We all try to improve the quality of our lives through the possessions we have, the places we go and the things we do. The most significant change to the quality of our life experience is going to come from changing our mental habits. The real pleasure of life comes from the peace and contentment of our minds, not the new car, or house, jewelry, new clothes, or the trip to Italy or some other country. Nor will the accomplishments from a life make the difference. These are all temporary changes that will leave us wanting.

There isn't anything we can do or have that will bring us greater joy and happiness than mastering being in the moment and controlling our thoughts/lower consciousness and actions. The peace and joy that comes from this is incredible.

How many times a day or week do you stop and appreciate what you have in your life that is good? There are many positive things in each of our lives. Just being on the planet and enjoying the many wonders that are here, should be enough, but we always want more. The lower consciousness is greedy, it can never be satisfied.

That wanting can be satisfied once and for all when we start the reprogramming process. The decision to be in the moment, be aware and control what we think about, will bring us more happiness and peace than anything else we can do, or from some possession we have. None of the things we do to satisfy our senses will bring long-term satisfaction.

Our effort to be happy is behind every decision we make. Our only goal in life is to be happy. So let's slow down and savor the gift of life as if it were an extremely expensive, delicious drink, or an incredible gourmet meal. Let us sip our way through life and enjoy all of the little things that make being alive so incredible. Let us capture the awe and splendor of our youth when simple little things brought us so much joy.

I use the knowledge of death to help me appreciate life. When I hear of some event that has ended someone's life, it pulls me back to the idea of how short a life really is and how it can end very suddenly.

When we are in the moment and living life purposely, the rewards are, being happy and being in a state of peace. Our lives are not random happenings subject to the whims of chance. We can control our minds and thoughts and live life deliberately and with purpose.

Being supported by one's mate in this endeavor to be in the moment and live purposely is really important. The person we spend a lot of time with can be either helpful or can make achieving this process harder. If your mate is one who makes this extremely difficult, then you are going to have an even more arduous task accomplishing these behavior changes. The same applies to relatives and friends who are a significant part of your life.

I am currently engaged to woman who is "on the path" as well, and it makes my goal to live in the moment so much easier. I have her to talk with about life and all of its challenges, and it makes it easier to deal with the many variables that confront us. She also helps me appreciate all of the little wonders of a day, such as the simple beauties and pleasures that go with being on the planet.

Many people are single and live alone. This can actually make these changes easier for you, as you do not have the distraction of another individual. Also, forming a group of friends to have discussions with can make this a much easier task. Getting back to the basics like family, friends, a good meal and the traditions of one's culture or religion can restore the simple beauty of life.

What if this was your last day of life on earth? What would you do? How would you spend that day? What if you had only six months to live? How would you live those last six months? What would you do or not do? It could just be your last six months, we do not know.

My ex-wife's mother was diagnosed with cancer and was told she had half-a-year at the most to live. At least she had a choice to live those last months as she wanted. Those six months could have been the best of her entire life.

My mother is going to be 90-years old in June of this year. My sister left the planet at age forty-three. We do not know what our karma has in store for us. We need to live life deliberately every day. We need to live everyday as if it were our last day on the planet, it just may well be.

I encourage you to take up meditating on a daily basis. Even if it is just for fifteen minutes per day, five days a week. If you have the time or inclination to spend more time, then do so. Try to make it part of your daily routine. Meditation will help you feel more connected to God and help you to feel a stronger connection to all that lives. Meditation is the key to accomplishing these mental behavior changes.

There is an internal peace that will be achieved when you are able to not listen to the lower consciousness' constant chatter.

Meditation will allow you to quiet the lower consciousness when it seems that it will just not shut up, even for a minute.

Every day on my drive to work I make an extra effort to stop thinking and appreciate the wonder of being a human being and the wonders that make up life's experience. To appreciate the simple little things, like a wave washing into shore, a tree waving in the wind or the fantastic colors and patterns of flowers. All of this is here for us to enjoy and it does not cost us anything. Life is so much richer when we appreciate the beauty of a day, whether the day is a rainy one, snowing, hot, cold, or one of those perfect California days we have so many of. What is more wonderful than to see a child smile or to hear them laugh?

REDEFINE YOURSELF

If you do not like the person you have become, why not consider making a change? I did it. I decided that I would like to be a different person, so I wrote out a description of the new me. I described this new person in great detail. It was not about how I looked, but who I was. I wanted to be a different person, to act differently.

Once I had the new description of this new person I wanted to be written out, I made reading it part of my daily routine. Every day while I was warming up my car for my drive to work, I would read the new description of me. I did this for many months, until I felt that I was this new person.

It was a simple reprogramming process. Just think, if you moved to a new location where no one knew you, they would have no idea of what kind of a person you were. They would have to learn everything about you from you. You would have the opportunity to be someone completely different. Why not save yourself the trouble of moving and just do it where you live now? We have the ability to make ourselves into anyone we want to be. We can be any way we want to be.

I have known many women who decided to get new friends, as the old ones were not enhancing their lives, but were, in fact, a drain on them. So they just discontinued associating with their old friends and made new ones.

Our lives are made up of a variety of many relationships with many different people. Some we can control and some we cannot. We may not be able to control the relationships we have at our work environment. Our relatives are our relatives; we cannot change them. We can decide if we want to make them a big part of our lives or not. We have the ability to choose the people who make up our world and the people we spend our time with.

I spend time with the individuals who enhance my life and no time with the people that take away from my life, bring negative energy, or create confusion.

This is an amazing experience we are a part of. Being a human being on the planet earth is so incredible. It seems to be very easy to forget about this or loose sight of the simple pleasures of life. It is so easy to take life for granted as well as so many of the other positive things that make up our lives.

With just a little effort everyday we can restore the wonder of the human experience. When we restore the wonder it makes everything that is a part of life richer. Our world is all in our minds.

EVERYTHING ABOUT LIFE IS AN IDEA!

CHANGE YOUR IDEAS, CHANGE YOUR LIFE.

<u>REMEMBER</u>:

Meditation is the key to concentration.

Concentration is the key to being in the moment.

Being in the moment is the key to being aware.

Being aware is the key to controlling the lower consciousness.

Controlling the lower consciousness is the key to controlling what we think about.

Controlling what we think about is the key to being happy.

Good Luck!

Have a great life – one moment at a time – one day at a time.

Love,
Arthur

_____

Appendix

Recommended reading:

Esoteric Buddhism, A.P. Sinnett

The Divine Art Of Living, Selections From The Baha't Writings

Wisdom Of The Mystic Masters, Joseph Weed

The Secret Of The Creative Vacuum, John Davidson

Spiritual Awakening, Darshan Singh

Path To Power, Roger Heisler

Esoteric Psychology II, Alice Bailey

The Power Of Now, Eckhart Tolle

The Voice Of The Silence, H.P. Blavatsky

Friendship With God, Neale Donald Walsch

Tao - The Subtle Universal Law and The Integral Way Of Life, Hua-Ching Ni

Self-Unfoldment, Disciplines Of Realization, Manly Hall

The Way Of The Kingdom,

The Philosopher's Stone, F. David Peat

The Secret Science Behind Miracles, Max Freedom Long

Secret Wisdom, David Conway

Perceiving Ordinary Magic, Science And Intuitive Wisdom, Jeromy Hayward

Vitality Energy Spirit, Thomas Cleary

Chaos, Making A New Science, James Gleick

The Essential Steiner, Rudolph Steiner

Conversations With God, Neale Donald Walsch

The Fourth Dimension, Charles Howard Hinton

The Experience Of No Self, Bernadette Roberts

A Way To Self Discovery, Ik Taimni

Kung Fu Meditations, Ellen Kei Hua

More Messages From Michael, Chelsea Guinn Yarbro

Lao Tzu, Tao Teachings, D.C. Lau

Sayings Of Uganda, Paramabansa Uganda

The Occult World, A.P. Sinnett

Reincarnation And Prayers To Live By, Jeanne Dixon

Simplified Magic, Ted Andrews

How To Know God, Swami Prabhavananda and Christopher Isherwood

Plato, The Republic and Other Works, .B. Jowett

The Meaning Of The Glorious Koran, Mohammed Marmaduke Pickthall

Light On The Path Through The Gates Of Gold, Mabel Collins

The Secret Doctrine, H.P. Blavatsky

Why I Am Not A Christian, Bertrand Russell

The Sermon On The Mount, Emmet Fox

The Koran, N.J. Dawood

The Supreme Adventure, Peter Hays

Studies In Occultism, H.P. Blavatsky

The Eagle's Quest, Fred Allen Wolfe

The Holy Bible

The Healing Runes, Ralph Blum and Susan Loughan

The Voice Of The Master, Kahlil Gibran

The Teaching Of Buddha, Bukkyo Dendo Kyokai

Space Time And Self, E. Norman Pearson

Man In Evolution, G. Depurucker

The Science Of Yoga, I.K. Taimni

The Goal And The Way, Swami Satprakashananda

The Secret Of Light, Walther Russell

The Aquarian Gospel Of Jesus The Christ, Levi

Third Series, Commentaries On Living, J. Krishnamurti

Illusions And Delusions Of The Supernatural And The Occult,
D.H. Rawcliffe

The Inner Life, Charles W. Ledbetter

White Sail, Thinley Norbu

Advanced Contemplation - The Peace Within You, Paul Brunton

The Science Of Being And Art Of Living, Maharishi Mahesh
Yogi

Fundamentals Of The Esoteric Philosophy, G. Depurucker

The Rosicrucian Cosmo Conception, Max Hindel

Transcendental Meditation, Blumfield-Cain-Jaffe

Magic, White And Black, Franz Hartman

Perspectives, The Timeless Ways Of Wisdom, Paul Brunton

The Fourth Way, P.D. Ouspensky

New Testament, Kwik Scan

The Rainbow In Your Hands, Albert Davis and Walter Rawls, Jr.

Sacred Science, R.A. Schwaller De Lubicz

Receiving The Cosmic Christ, Shahan Jon

Isis Unveiled, H.P. Blavatsky

The Book Of Mormon

Zen And Japanese Culture, Daisetz Suzuki

The Late Great Planet Earth, Hal Lindsy

Colour Meditations, S.G.J. Ouseley

Zen In The Art Of Archery, Eugene Herrigel

The Song Of God, Bhagavad-Gita

The Lost Years Of Jesus Revealed, Reverend Dr. Charles Francis
Potter

The Elements Of Style, William Strunk Jr. and E.B. White

The Method Of Zen, Eugene Herrigel

The Kamasutra Of Vatsayana, Sir Richard Burton and F.F.
Arbuthnot

Nietzche Thus Spoke Zarathustra, Walter Kaufman

The Tibetan Book Of The Dead, W.Y. Evans-Wentz

Recovering The Soul, Larry Dossey

The Art Of Joyful Living, Swami Rama

Psychic Energy, M.Esther Harding

Return Of The Reshi, Depack Chopra

The Prophet, Kahlil Gibran

The Bhagavadgita In The Mahabharata, J.A.B. Van Buitenen

The Great Initiates, Edouard Schure

Masterpieces Of World Philosophy, Frank N. Magill

From Socrates To Sartre; The Philosophic Quest, T.Z. Levine

The Art Of Being And Becoming, Hazart Inayat Khan

Returning To Silence, Dainin Katagiri

Cosmic Consciousness, Richard Bucke

The World Treasure Of Modern Religious Thought, Jaroslav Pelican

The Celestine Prophecy, James Redfield

Mohandas K. Ghandi, an Autobiography, translated By Mahadev Desai

A History Of Western Philosophy, Bertrand Russell

Workbook For Spiritual Development Of All People, Hua-Ching Ni

Joyful Path Of Good Fortune, Geshe Kelsang Gyatso

Enlightened Mind Devine Mind, Paul Brunton

Creative Meditation And Multidimensional Consciousness, Lama Anagarika Govinda

The Vision Dhamma, Nyanaponika Thera

The Varieties Of Religious Experience, William James

The Study Of Consciousness, Annie Basant

Homage To The Sun, Kyriacos Markides

Frontiers Of The Soul, Michael Grosso

Soul Mates, Thomas Moore

Self And Liberation, Daniel Meckel And Robert Moore

Seat Of The Soul, Gary Zukav

Bodymind, Ken Dychtwald

The Undiscovered Self, C.G. Jung

Life Of Christ, Bishop Fulton Sheen

Connections To The World, Arthur Danto

Only Love Is Real, Brian Weiss

The Accent Of Self, B.N. Parimoo

Ancient Wisdom And Modern Science, Stanislav Grof

The Story Of Philosophy, Willima Durant

The Experience Of Light, Joseph Goldstien

Zen Rock Gardening, Moore

Wen-Tzu, Understanding The Mysteries, Further Teaching Of
Lau-Tzu, Thomas Cleary

The Science Of Alura, L.G.J. Ouseley

Life And Teaching Of The Masters Of The Far East, Baird
Spalding

Earth Power, Scott Cunningham

The Finding Of The Third Eye, Vera Stanley Alder

Chinese Thought, An Introduction, Donald Bishop